BARBARA ROSSI

DESTINATION ANIME!

AN ANIME LOVER'S GUIDE TO TOKYO

SAN RAFAEL • LOS ANGELES • LONDON

PO Box 3088
San Rafael, CA 94912
www.insighteditions.com

Find us on Facebook: www.facebook.com/InsightEditions
Follow us on Instagram: @insighteditions

This work was originally published by Éditions Kappalab as *Anime Tour, pellegrinaggio nei luoghi cult dell'animazione giapponese.* Originally published in French as *Destination [illegible] Voyage au Japon à travers l'animation!* by Ynnis Éditions, France, in 2024.

English translation by Andie Ho.

ISBN: 979-8-33740-054-9

Publisher: Raoul Goff

SVP, Co-Publisher: Vanessa Lopez

VP, Creative: Chrissy Kwasnik

VP, Manufacturing: Alix Nicholaeff

Editorial Director: Lia Brown

Art Director: Matt Girard

Designer: Allister Fein

Senior Editor: Stephen Fall

Editorial Assistant: Audrey Salo

Executive Managing Editor: Maria Spano

Senior Production Manager: Greg Steffen

Strategic Production Planner: Lina s Palma-Temena

c/o Ynnis Éditions
38 rue Notre-Dame-de-Nazareth
75003 PARIS
https://ynnis-editions.fr

YnnisÉditions
@Ynnis_Editions

President: Cedric Littardi
Editorial manager: Sébastien Rost
French edition: Charlotte Thomas
Editorial coordinator: Jeanne Bucher
Revisions: Julien Picquart
Layout: Camille Pradère
Printing: centSucres
Marketing & communications: Alexandra Sacone

Original photography by Barbara Rossi, Alessandro Nalli, Andi Winata, Cem Ersozlu, Wencheng Jiang, John Gillespie, Maeda Akihiko, Antonio Tajuelo, Gregory Lane, Jake Images, Kazzpix, Mos Design, Luke Ma, Nikolay Likomanov, Jieun Kim, Tunafish, Ryoji Iwata, Andy Kuo, Mister0124, mk623, Syoko Matsumura, Ocdp, Shiro Ang, Sou, Asturio Cantabrio, Wiiii, Atul Vinayak, Rsa, Vista Wei, つ, Xillian Justen de Vasconcellos, Wally Gobetz, Manuel Velasquez, Sabrina, Christoph Theisinger, Giuseppe Milo, Dennis Amith, Aleksandar Pasaric, B Lucava, Wpcpey, Trevor Dobson, Denys Nevozhai, hans-johnson, Kakidai, Arashiyama, Timo Voltz, Minseong Kim, Jezael Melgoza, Ananda Raihan, Kvinga, ペン太, Caito, Kentaro Toma, Szymon Shields, Syced, JordyMeow, Asanagi, Victor Deweerdt, HONCHAN, ys-energy, Guilhem Vellut, そらみみ, Nearby Tokyo, Raita Futo, Kone, Morio, Suikotei, Kentaro Ohno, Kazuhr, Asanagi, or-kame, Pexels, Unsplash, Wikimedia commons, Pixta, Flickr

Insight Editions, in association with Roots of Peace, will plant two trees for each tree used in the manufacturing of this book. Roots of Peace is an internationally renowned humanitarian organization dedicated to eradicating land mines worldwide and converting war-torn lands into productive farms and wildlife habitats. Roots of Peace will plant two million fruit and nut trees in Afghanistan and provide farmers there with the skills and support necessary for sustainable land use.

Manufactured in China by Insight Editions

10 9 8 7 6 5 4 3 2 1

CONTENTS

INTRODUCTION

The book in your hands is dedicated to all the fans of Japanese animation who dream of visiting the Land of the Rising Sun at least once in their lives—those who grew up with ***Dragon Ball***, *Sailor Moon*, ***Urusei Yatsura***, ***Evangelion***, and so many more. This guide takes you on a journey to discover the real-life places that inspired your favorite anime. Japanese animation has gained popularity well beyond its homeland, and many fans find themselves wishing they could experience firsthand the landmarks and locations that serve as backdrops for their beloved films and series. Perhaps you are inspired to experience more than the average tourist and to take a closer look at the streets and buildings of Japan to figure out why they feel so familiar.

Be forewarned, however: This book is not intended as a comprehensive travel guide. You won't find a list of popular attractions or instructions for buying metro tickets. Instead, it is an additional resource to take with you on your visits to more traditional tourist spots.

If you find yourself in **Shinjuku**, you need only to look around or veer off the beaten path to come across places featured in *City Hunter: Shinjuku Private Eyes* or *Your Name.* In **Shibuya**, you might recognize locations from *Death Note*, and in **Roppongi**, you'll see many of the settings for *Sailor Moon*. Outside the sprawling metropolis of Tokyo, we go in search of **Totoro**'s forest among the hills of **Saitama**.

Next, we take a trip down memory lane through **Nerima**, the birthplace of anime, to places depicted in *Inuyasha*, *Ranma ½* and *Creamy Mami, the Magical Angel*. We also take a quick spin around the sites that inspired *Demon Slayer*.

INSTRUCTIONS

This book makes it quick and easy to find points of interest using any GPS-enabled device:

A. Each section is dedicated to a particular movie, a series, or a point of interest featuring multiple characters (including the final section on Nerima).

B. Each section is color coded and contains a map with numbered location markers.

C. Each map also features pink location markers with letters. These markers are pink in every section and identify recurring points of interest (such as Tokyo Tower) that appear as backdrops or settings for plot points. At the end of the book is a complete list of these places, with a brief description of each.

For convenience, the coordinates (latitude and longitude) are provided for each site so that you can locate them using an app such as **Google Maps**, available for smartphones. This will help you pinpoint exact locations and vistas—like a scavenger hunt! Using a brief web search, you can look up a business's hours of operation or reserve a table at a restaurant—even the one where Kaori and Ryo (*City Hunters*) dined. The goal of this book is to offer a unique, extensive anime tour of Japan, for spectacular memories to cherish until your next trip!

1

A

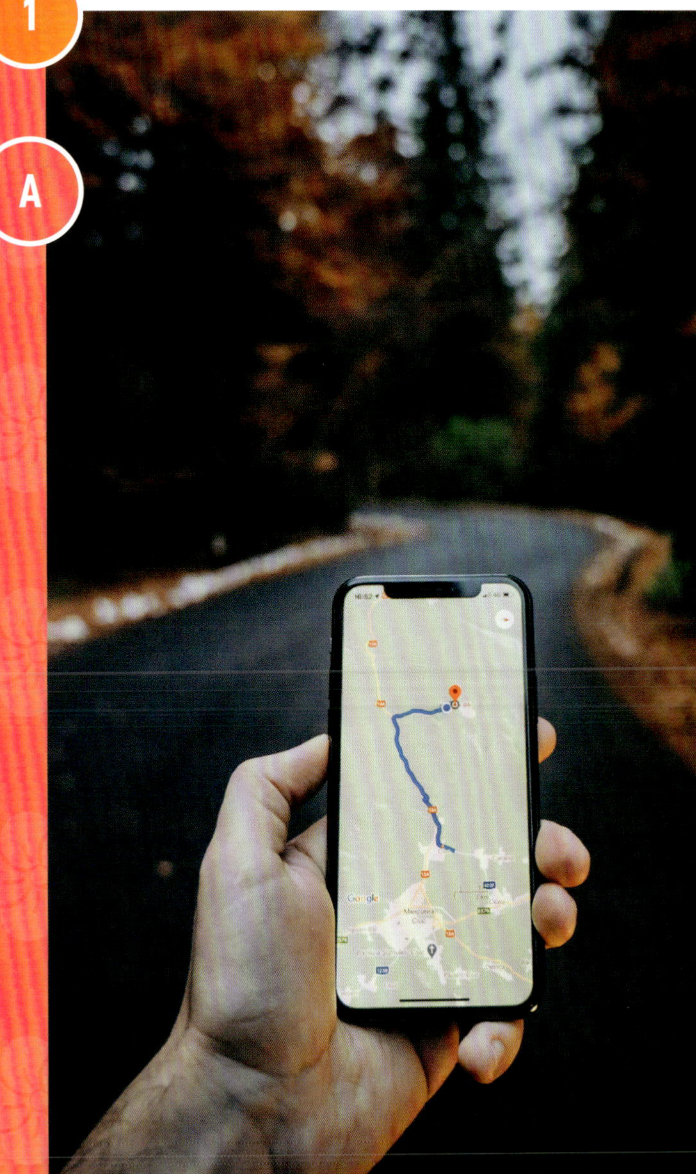

Scan Me!

YOUR NAME.

Your Name. follows the intertwined lives of Mitsuha, a girl from the tiny mountain town of Itomori, and Taki, a boy from the vibrant city of Tokyo. Although the two are complete strangers, they find their destinies linked when they mysteriously wake up in each other's bodies. Using notes, messages, and clues, they begin to communicate and leave breadcrumbs for one another. Just as they start to adapt to the strange phenomenon, their connection abruptly vanishes, prompting Taki to embark on a quest to find Mitsuha.

Taki's journey takes him through some of Tokyo's most iconic districts, including Shinjuku, Shibuya, and Minato. Director Makoto Shinkai captures these parts of the city so vividly that viewers familiar with Tokyo will recognize the film's scenery and ambiance.

Mitsuha's story, set in the Gifu region, is equally well detailed, with Shinkai's inspiration drawn from real locations that fans can easily recognize and visit.

YOUR NAME.
MAKOTO SHINKAI (2016)

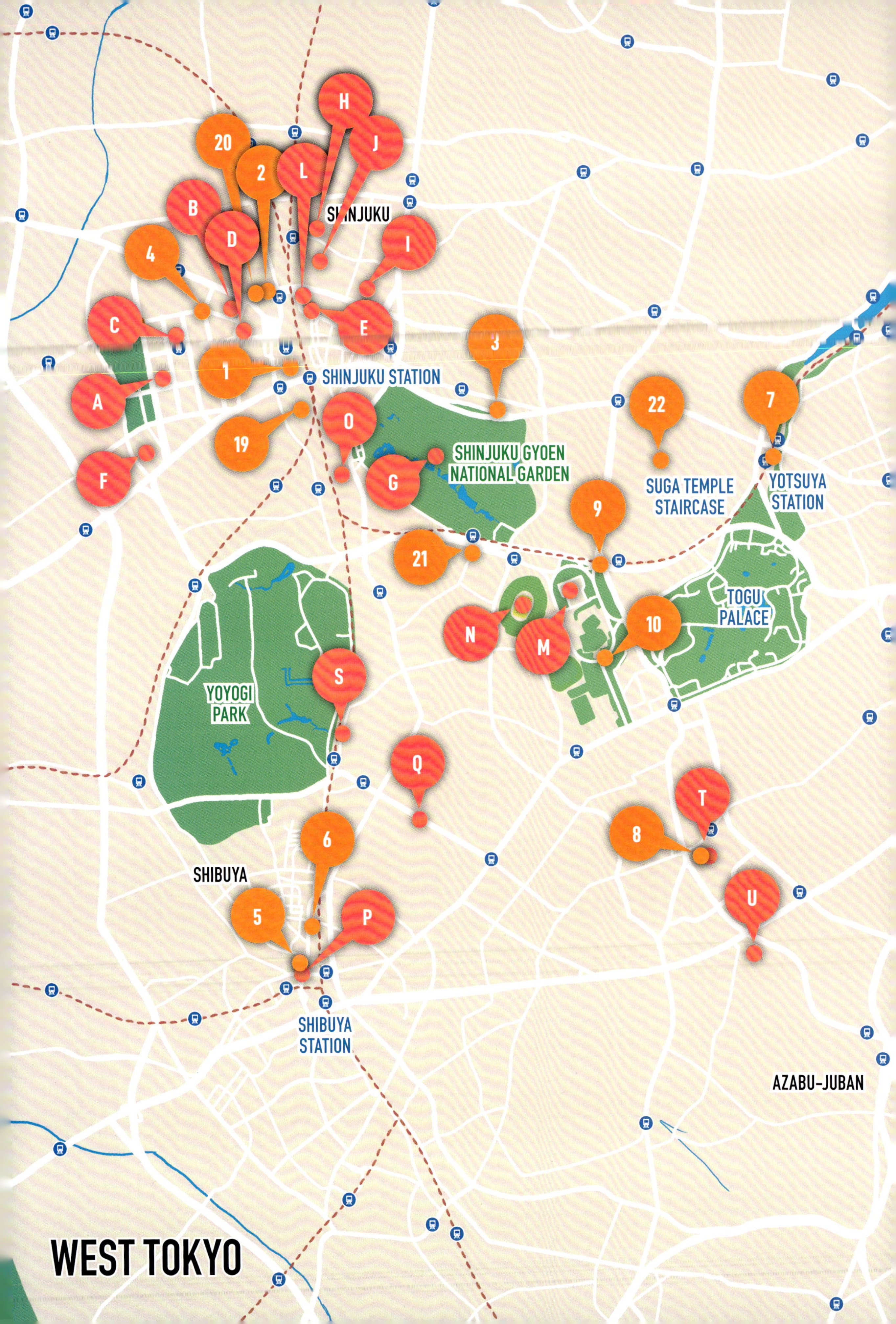
WEST TOKYO
SHINJUKU
SHINJUKU STATION
SHINJUKU GYOEN NATIONAL GARDEN
SUGA TEMPLE STAIRCASE
YOTSUYA STATION
TOGU PALACE
YOYOGI PARK
SHIBUYA
SHIBUYA STATION
AZABU-JUBAN
20
2
4
1
19
3
22
7
9
21
10
6
5
8
H
J
L
B
D
I
C
E
A
O
G
F
N
M
S
Q
T
U
P

EAST TOKYO
HIDA
17
11
JR TOKYO STATION
13
16
15
14
V
TOKYO TOWER
18
12
JAPAN
IWATE
SAKATA
YAMAGATA
SENDAI
NIIGATA
NIIGATA
FUKUSHIMA
FUKUSHIMA
ISHIKAWA
KANAZAWA
NAGANO
GUNMA
TOCHIJI
FUKUI
GIFU
SAITAMA
IBARAKI
TOTTORI
SHIMANE
OKAYAMA
HYOGO
KYOTO
YAMANASHI
TOKYO
YOKOHAMA
CHIBA
HIROSHIMA
YAMAGUCHI
OSAKA
AICHI
FUKUOKA
KAGAWA
MATSUYAMA
NARA
MIE
SAGA
TOKUSHIMA
EHIME
KOCHI
WAKAYAMA
OITA
KOCHI

1

JR SHINJUKU STATION
SOUTH ENTRANCE

SHINJUKU

COORDINATES
35.68963, 139.70179

2

SUNFLOWER BUILDING

SHINJUKU

COORDINATES
35.69338, 139.69881

L

YUNIKA VISION

SHINJUKU

COORDINATES
35.69342, 139.70063

D

TOKYO MODE GAKUEN

SHINJUKU

COORDINATES
35.69166, 139.69694

3

CAFÉ LA BOHEME

SHINJUKU

COORDINATES
35.68753, 139.71283

WEBSITE
www.boheme.jp/shinjuku-gyoen

4

KITA DORI INTERSECTION

SHINJUKU

COORDINATES
35.69259, 139.6944

0

NTT DOCOMO YOYOGI TOWER

SHIBUYA

COORDINATES
35.6844, 139.70308

V

TOKYO TOWER
MINATO

COORDINATES
35.65858, 139.74543

5

STARBUCKS COFFEE
SHIBUYA

COORDINATES
35.65985, 139.70035

B

SOMPO BUILDING
SHINJUKU

COORDINATES
35.69272, 139.69611

6

TOWER RECORDS
SHIBUYA

COORDINATES
35.66191, 139.70099

7

JR YOTSUYA STATION
SHINJUKU

COORDINATES
35.68532, 139.72978

U

ROPPONGI HILLS MORI TOWER
MINATO

COORDINATES
35.66073, 139.729

8

CAFÉ COQUILLE
MINATO

COORDINATES
35.6648, 139.72631

WEBSITE
www.hiramatsurestaurant.jp/nacc-coquille

9 SHINANOMACHI FOOTBRIDGE
SHINJUKU

COORDINATES
35.67947, 139.71965

10 CROSSWALK
SHINJUKU

COORDINATES
35.67529, 139.7196

11 JR TOKYO STATION
CHIYODA

COORDINATES
35.68123, 139.76712

12 NAGOYA STATION
SHINJUKU

COORDINATES
35.17091, 136.88153

13 HIDA-FURUKAWA STATION
GIFU

COORDINATES
36.23672, 137.1896

14 KETA WAKAMIYA SHRINE
GIFU

COORDINATES
36.23948, 137.19782

WEBSITE
www.gifu-jinjacho.jp

15 AJIDOKORO FURUKAWA
GIFU

COORDINATES
36.23575, 137.18521

WEBSITE
www.ajidokoro.jp

16

HIDA LIBRARY

GIFU

COORDINATES

36.23806, 137.18554

17

OCHIAI BUS STOP

GIFU

COORDINATES

36.30343, 137.11273

18

OKUOOI GUESTHOUSE

SHIZUOKA

COORDINATES

35.15161, 138.1463

WEBSITE

www.minshukuokuooi.jp

19

STARBUCKS COFFEE, SOUTHERN TERRACE

SHINJUKU

COORDINATES

35.68796, 139.70028

20

SHINTOSHIN FOOTBRIDGE

SHINJUKU

COORDINATES

35.69336, 139.69731

21

JR SENDAGAYA STATION

SHIBUYA

COORDINATES

35.68119, 139.71128

22

SUGA TEMPLE STAIRCASE

SHINJUKU

COORDINATES

35.68509, 139.72333

JR SHINJUKU STATION, SOUTH ENTRANCE

Mitsuha exits JR Shinjuku station via the **South Entrance** and encounters the stunning sight of this bustling street winding between the skyscrapers. For the full experience, head up to the footbridge that runs alongside the station. The **bus terminal** is visible in the photo below.

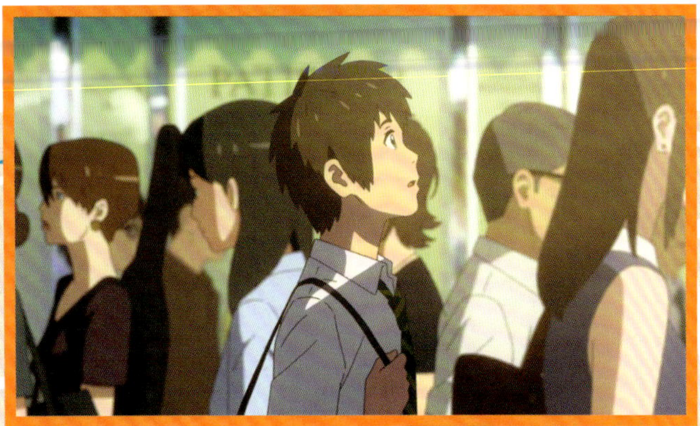

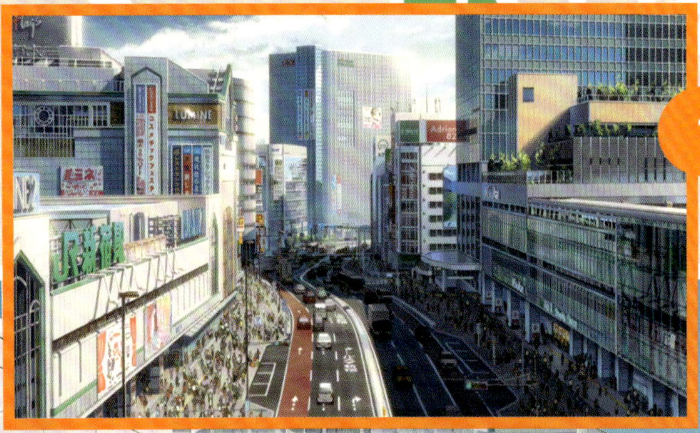

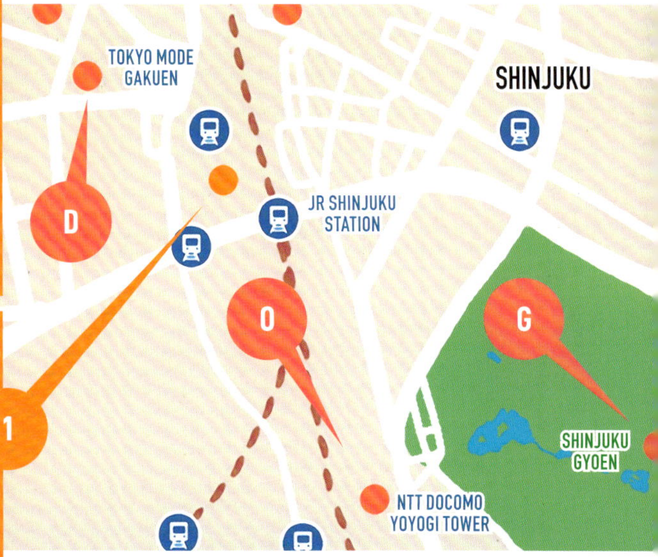

TOKYO MODE GAKUEN

SHINJUKU

D

JR SHINJUKU STATION

O

G

1

SHINJUKU GYOEN

NTT DOCOMO YOYOGI TOWER

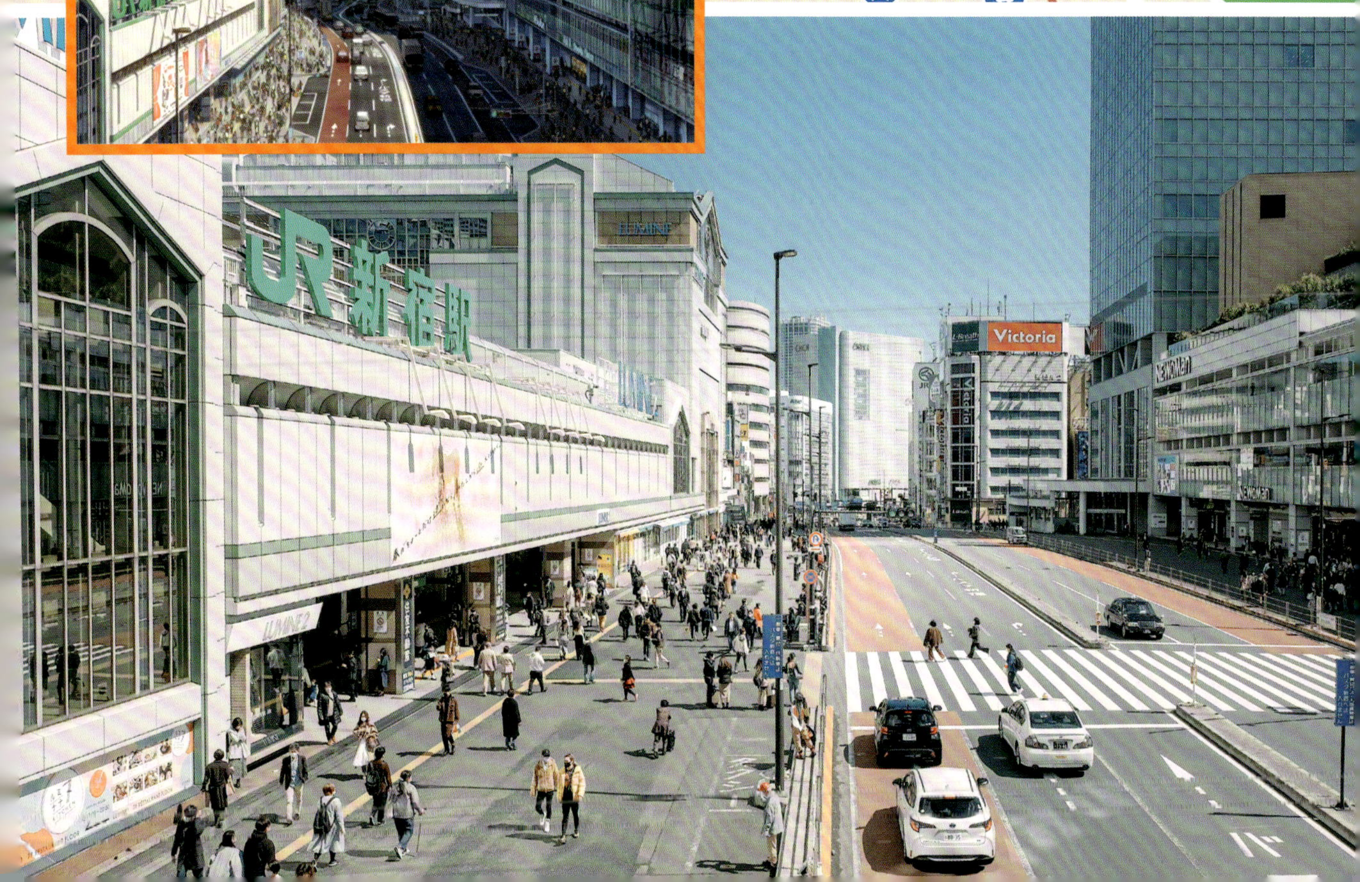

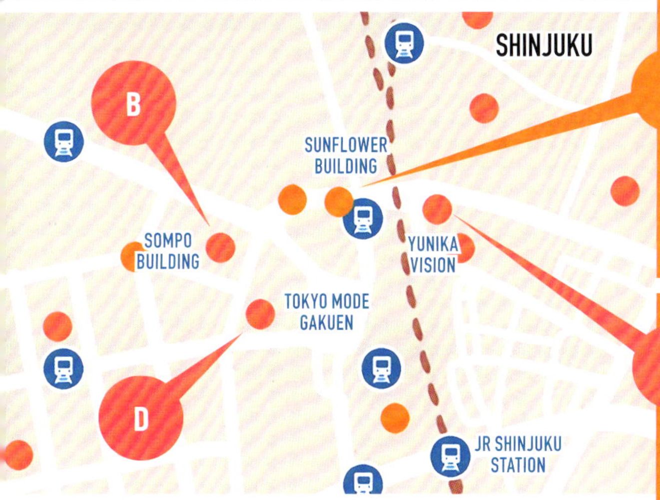

SHINJUKU

SUNFLOWER BUILDING

SOMPO BUILDING

YUNIKA VISION

TOKYO MODE GAKUEN

JR SHINJUKU STATION

AROUND SHINJUKU STATION

These buildings might look familiar to you, as they appear often in the film as well as in other works by Shinkai. The images to the right show (from top to bottom) the intersection outside the Sunflower Building, the Yunika Vision sign, and a view of Tokyo Mode Gakuen (also known as Cocoon Tower) from the Yunika Vision intersection when facing the East Entrance of Shinjuku Station.

CAFÉ LA BOHEME

Taki has a part-time job working evenings as a waiter at a charming restaurant called the **Garden of Words** (a nod to Shinkai's film of the same name), which overlooks Shinjuku Gyoen National Garden. The closest public transit stop is the Shinjuku-gyoemmae metro station.

INTERSECTION OF KITA DORI, NTT DOCOMO YOYOGI TOWER & TOKYO TOWER

The Kita Dori intersection and Yoyogi and Tokyo Towers all make frequent cameos in Shinkai's works. In *Your Name.*, they symbolize the passage of time. In the background are three of the most iconic skyscrapers in Shinjuku: the Sompo Building, the Sumitomo Building, and Tokyo Mode Gakuen (Cocoon Tower).

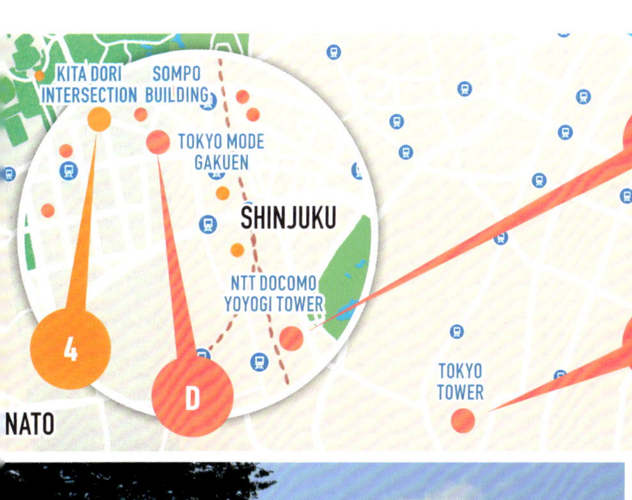

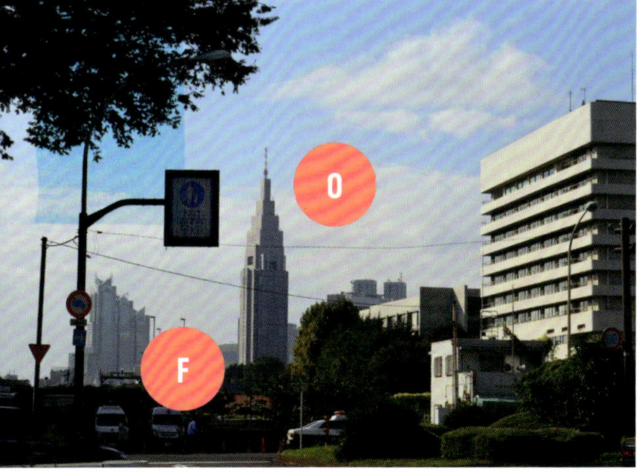

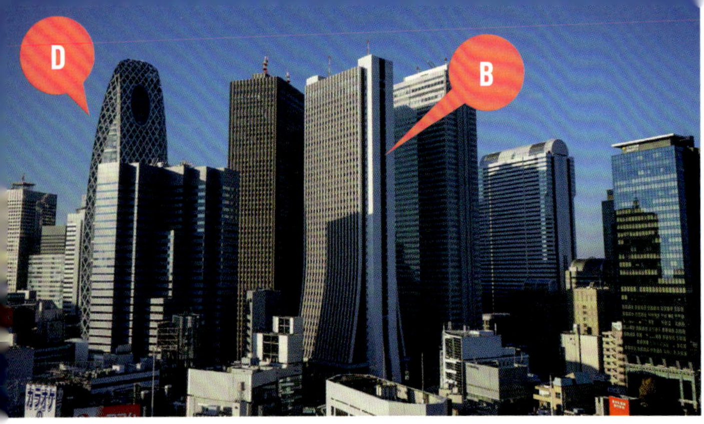

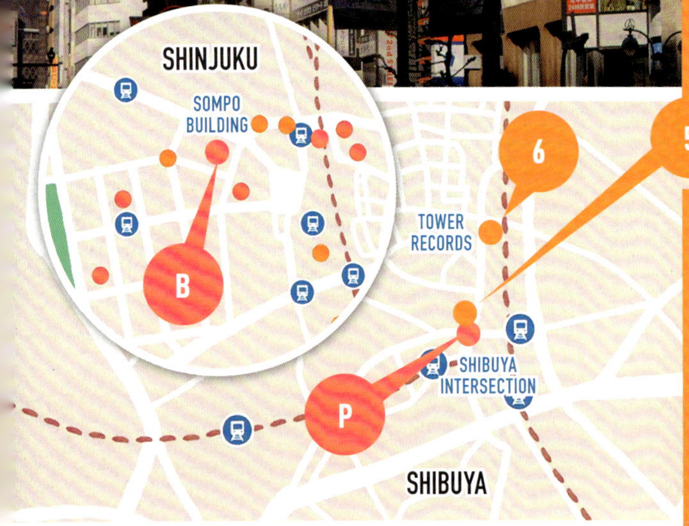

STARBUCKS COFFEE, SOMPO BUILDING & TOWER RECORDS SHIBUYA

Other glimpses of Tokyo include Taki and Miki at Starbucks Coffee (top) at the intersection in front of Shibuya Station. In the center and bottom images, Taki walks past the Sompo Building in Shinjuku and the Tower Records store in Shibuya.

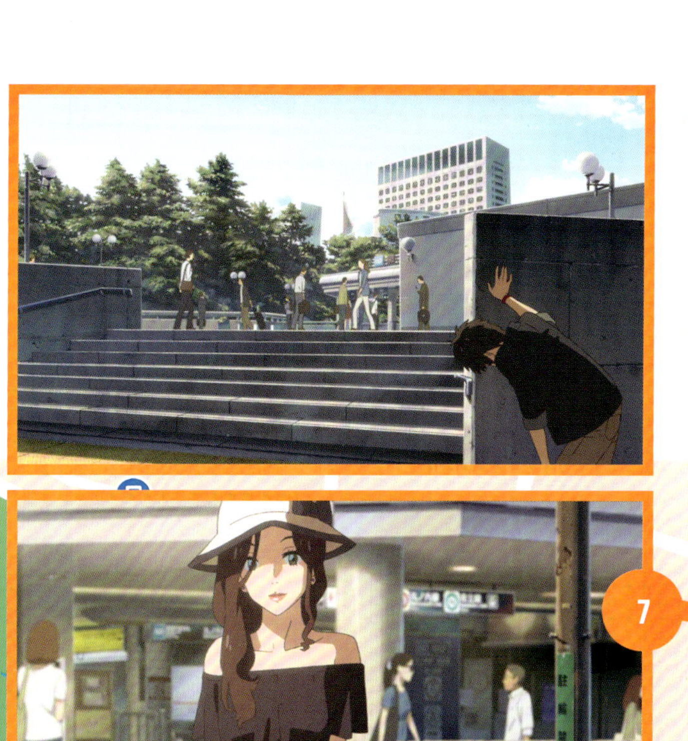

JR YOTSUYA STATION

Miki and Taki meet at **Yotsuya Station**, where the Marunouchi metro line and the JR Chuo railway line converge. Both are heavily used by suburban residents, especially the JR Chuo Line, which runs through the entire city of Tokyo.

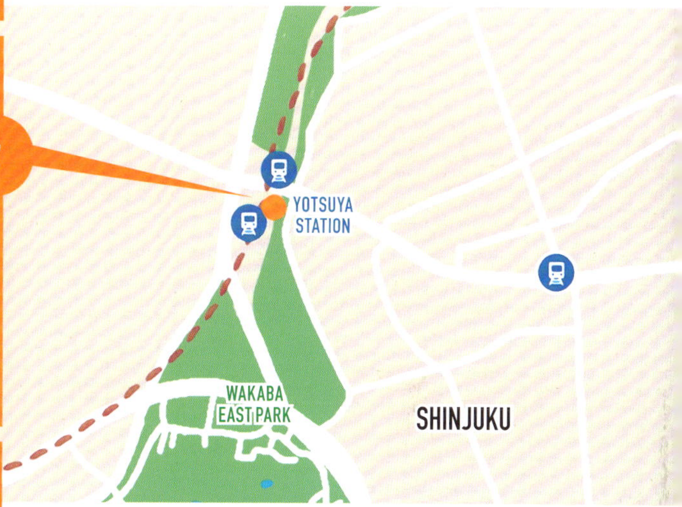

ROPPONGI HILLS MORI TOWER & CAFÉ COQUILLE (NACT)

After visiting the panoramic observatory at Mori Tower, Taki and Miki stop for a snack at Café Coquille inside the National Art Center Tokyo (NACT). The café features a 70-foot ceiling and unique architecture. It's well worth a visit and, as Taki and Miki found, a great spot for a quick bite.

SHINANOMACHI FOOTBRIDGE & CROSSWALK

The Shinanomachi footbridge connects **Shinanomachi Station** to the park adjoining the **Meiji Memorial Museum**. Taki takes the bridge often, crossing it several times in the film; Mitsuha does the same on her search for Taki in Tokyo. At the edge of the park, just before the tree-lined avenue, is the crosswalk that Taki and his friends take every day to get to school. The school they attend does not seem to correspond to any actual building.

JR TOKYO STATION

The JR Tokyo Station is a major railway hub, with bullet trains (*shinkansen*) departing for destinations across the country. The JR Tokyo Station is in Chiyoda and serves the East Japan Railway Company (JR East) lines, the Central Japan Railway Company (JR Tokai) lines, and the Marunouchi metro line.

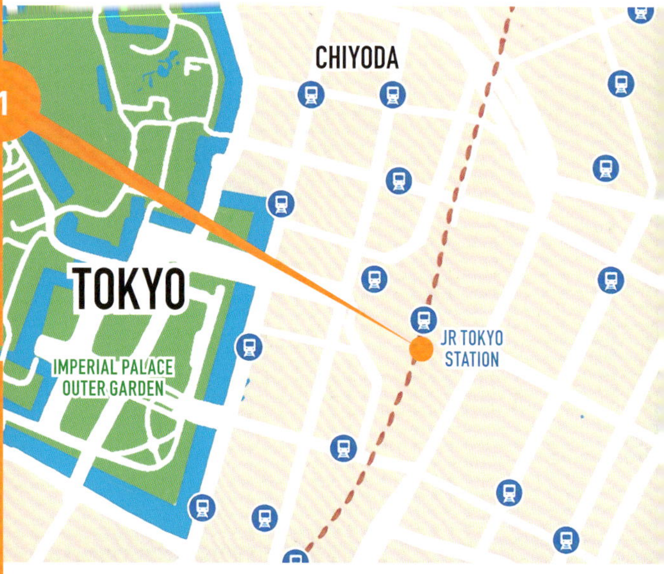

CHIYODA

11

TOKYO

IMPERIAL PALACE OUTER GARDEN

JR TOKYO STATION

Located in the heart of the business district, **JR Tokyo Station** connects directly to buildings that house the numerous offices in the area. The buildings are also accessible via an underground shopping center that connects to the station and features shops selling merchandise from popular anime films.

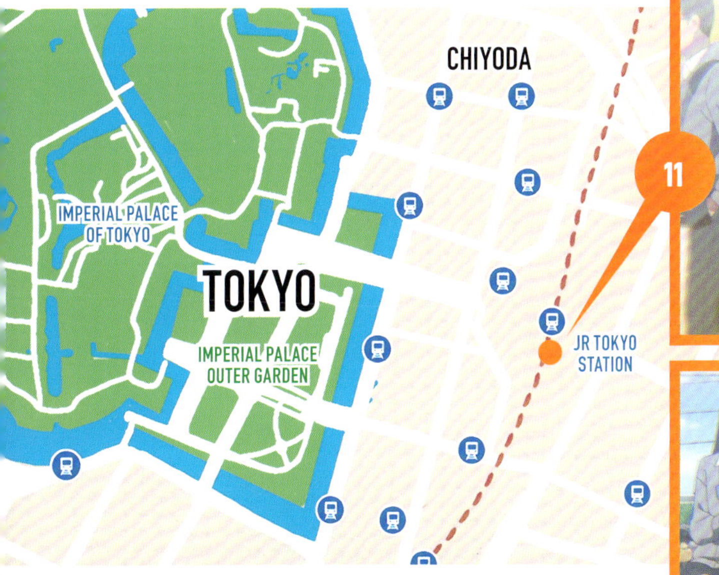

CHIYODA

IMPERIAL PALACE OF TOKYO

TOKYO

IMPERIAL PALACE OUTER GARDEN

11

JR TOKYO STATION

NAGOYA STATION

In a different timeline from Mitsuha's, Taki and his friends journey toward Itomori. In Nagoya, they switch from the bullet train to a local train on Tokai's Takayama line.

HIDA-FURUKAWA STATION

Taki's travels end at the small Hida-Furukawa Station, where he and his friends begin their search for Mitsuha. Taki gradually uncovers the truth about what happened in the past.

KETA WAKAMIYA SHRINE

The film takes license with its depiction of the Keta Wakamiya Shrine, commonly called Itomori Temple, but it's still worth a visit if you happen to be in the area. Many a *Your Name.* fan has left behind an *ema*, a small wooden plaque engraved with a prayer.

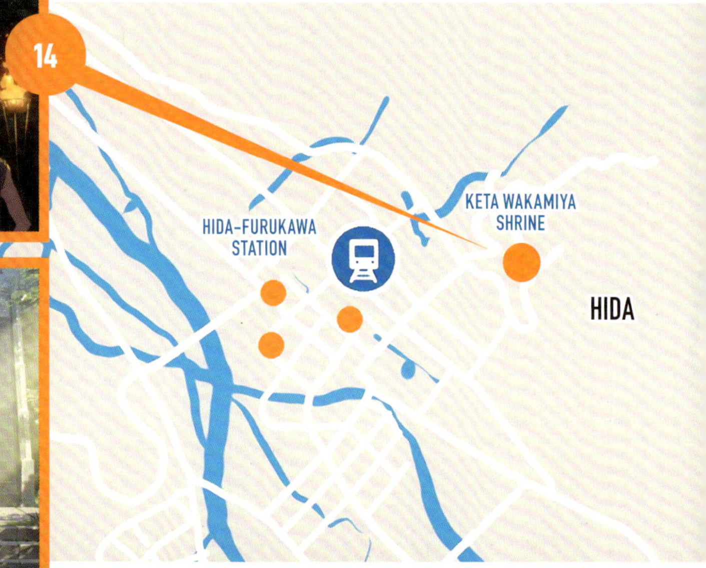

14

HIDA-FURUKAWA STATION

KETA WAKAMIYA SHRINE

HIDA

AJIDOKORO FURUKAWA

This souvenir shop and its small adjoining restaurant differ slightly from the location depicted in the film, but it's still a favorite stop for fans because of its excellent *goheimochi*, which Miki and Tsukasa eat in the movie. The shop sells *Your Name.* souvenirs, including maps with locations from the film and even sake. Although it isn't the *kuchikamizake* sake from the movie, the drink has been blessed by monks from Keta Wakamiya Shrine.

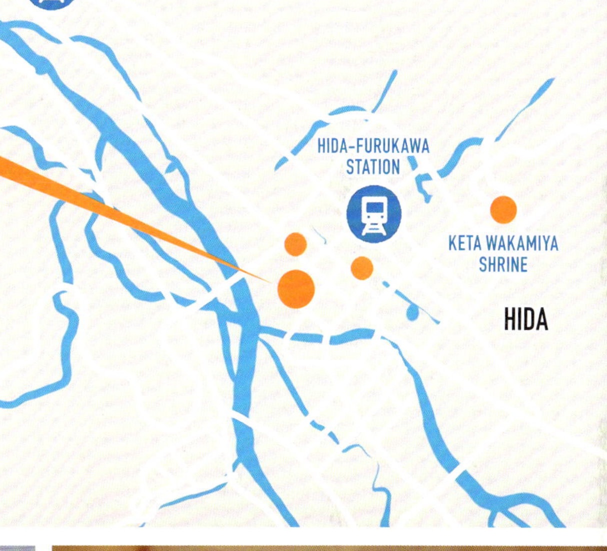

17

HIDA CITY LIBRARY & OCHIAI BUS STOP

The library is just a few minutes' walk from the train station, and although the exterior looks different from the movie, the inside is the same. The bus stop where the boys sit is no longer served, but it remains a landmark for fans of the film.

16

17

OCHIAI BUS STOP

HIDA-FURUKAWA STATION

HIDA

17

16

OKUOOI GUESTHOUSE

Sadly, the restaurant in Takayama where the boys enjoy their ramen doesn't actually exist. However, the guesthouse in Itomori where Taki, Miki, and Tsukasa spend the night was inspired by a real place not in Hida, but in Shizuoka Prefecture.

19

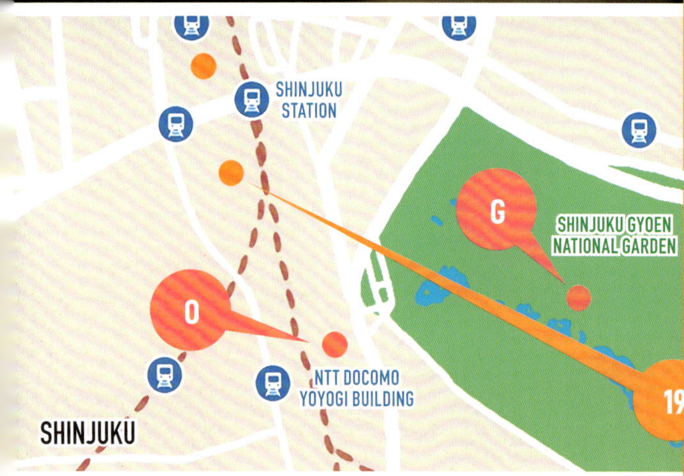

SHINJUKU STATION

SHINJUKU GYOEN NATIONAL GARDEN

G

O

NTT DOCOMO YOYOGI BUILDING

19

SHINJUKU

STARBUCKS COFFEE, SOUTHERN TERRACE

South of JR Shinjuku Station is Shinjuku Southern Terrace, a retail complex with four stories of shops and restaurants. There's something for everyone here, but the location is known for its holiday lights that create an enchanting atmosphere.

SHINTOSHIN FOOTBRIDGE

From the Shintoshin footbridge, you can see the **Sompo Building** and its unique flared base.

JR SENDAGAYA STATION

When they spot each other through the train windows, Taki and Mitsuha get off at their stations in Shinjuku and Sendagaya and walk to the **Suga Temple Staircase**. Their routes are shown on the next page.

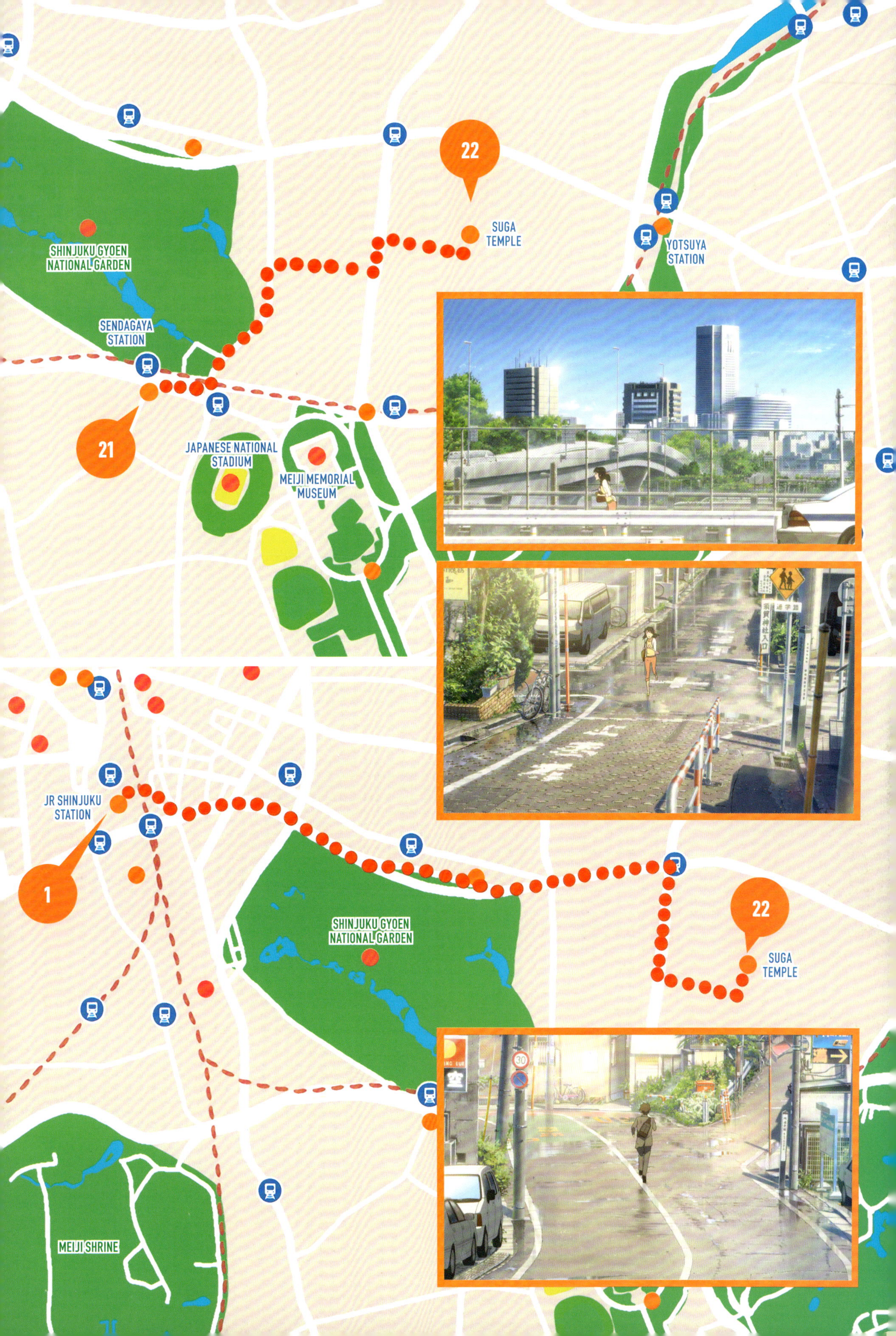
22
SUGA TEMPLE
SHINJUKU GYOEN NATIONAL GARDEN
YOTSUYA STATION
SENDAGAYA STATION
21
JAPANESE NATIONAL STADIUM
MEIJI MEMORIAL MUSEUM
JR SHINJUKU STATION
1
SHINJUKU GYOEN NATIONAL GARDEN
22
SUGA TEMPLE
MEIJI SHRINE

SUGA TEMPLE STAIRCASE

The staircase has become a famous landmark on ***Your Name.*** tours. At the top of the stairs is **Suga Temple**, a peaceful place of prayer in the heart of the bustling Shinjuku district.

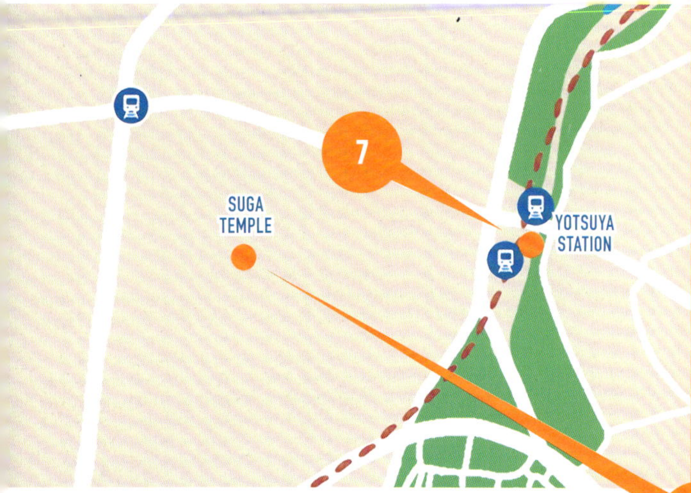

CITY HUNTER

Ryo Saeba and Kaori Makimura are contacted by a young woman in distress: Ai Shindo, a model and medical student. Ai is being pursued by dangerous individuals searching for a mysterious key to a secret mind-controlled weapon that Ai's father had been developing before he was murdered. Shinji Mikuni, Ai's childhood friend and the powerful owner of a multinational communications company, also seems to be involved. The plot unfolds around the struggle to protect Ai and uncover the truth about the weapon through intrigue, plot twists, and dark secrets.

The action takes place entirely in Shinjuku, as do all the stories (both in print and on screen) that feature Ryo Saeba, the self-proclaimed "Stallion of Shinjuku." This adventure focuses on the **Kabukicho** district ("the district that never sleeps") and the **Golden Gai** area, a can't-miss stop for authentic Japanese nightlife. The final battle in the movie involves the hero Ryo and the imposing Umibozu in **Shinjuku Gyoen National Garden**.

CITY HUNTER: SHINJUKU PRIVATE EYES

KENJI KODAMA (2019)

SHIN
SHINJUKU GYOEN NATIONAL GARDEN
MEIJI SHRINE GARDEN
YOYOGI PARK
SHIBUYA
JR SHIBUYA STATION
WEST TOKYO

EAST TOKYO
IMPERIAL PALACE
OUTER GARDEN
4
CHUO
JR SHIMBASHI
STATION
V
TOKYO TOWER
HAMARIKYU
GARDENS
AZABU-JUBAN STATION
MINATO
SHIBAURA-FUTO
STATION
W
RAINBOW BRIDGE
X
Y
DAIKANRANSHA
FERRIS WHEEL
ODAIBA-KAIHINKÔEN
STATION

1 DON QUIJOTE

SHINJUKU

COORDINATES
35.6938, 139.70176

WEBSITE
www.donki.com

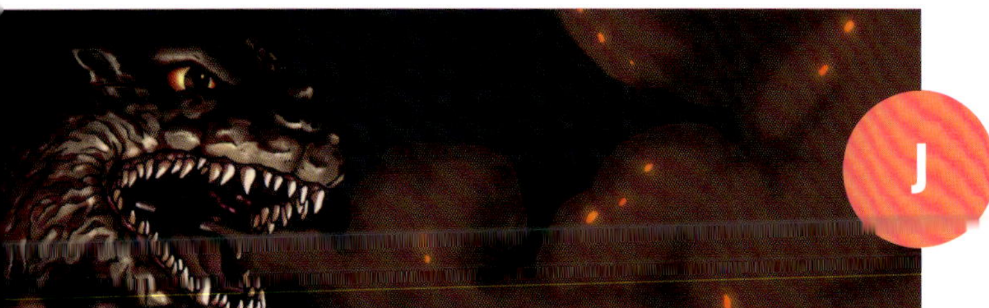

J GODZILLA STATUE

SHINJUKU

COORDINATES
35.69505, 139.70191

WEBSITE
www.toho.co.jp

2 JR SHINJUKU STATION, EAST ENTRANCE / LUMINE EST

SHINJUKU

COORDINATES
35.69199, 139.70102

3 JR SHINJUKU STATION, SOUTH ENTRANCE

SHINJUKU

COORDINATES
35.68963, 139.70179

A METROPOLITAN GOVERNMENT BUILDING

SHINJUKU

COORDINATES
35.68948, 139.69168

WEBSITE
www.metro.tokyo.lg.jp

D TOKYO MODE GAKUEN

SHINJUKU

COORDINATES
35.69166, 139.69694

C SUMITOMO BUILDING

SHINJUKU

COORDINATES
35.69135, 139.69261

4 METROPOLITAN POLICE HEADQUARTERS

CHIYODA

COORDINATES
35.67714, 139.7523

5 NEW YORK GRILL

SHINJUKU

COORDINATES
35.68531, 139.69101

6 HANAZONO SHRINE

SHINJUKU

COORDINATES
35.69353, 139.70532

W RAINBOW BRIDGE

MINATO

COORDINATES
35.63656, 139.76314

X FUJI TELEVISION NETWORK

MINATO

COORDINATES
35.6266, 139.77405

7 ISETAN DEPARTMENT STORE

SHINJUKU

COORDINATES
35.69157, 139.70464

WEBSITE
www.mistore.jp

8 SUBNADE SHOPPING CENTER

SHINJUKU

COORDINATES
35.69338, 139.70208

WEBSITE
www.subnade.co.jp

I

GOLDEN GAI

SHINJUKU

COORDINATES
35.69411, 139.70476

WEBSITE
goldengai.jp

F

SHINJUKU PARK TOWER

SHINJUKU

COORDINATES
35.68542, 139.69083

WEBSITE
www.shinjukuparktower.com

9

SHINJUKU BUS TERMINAL

SHINJUKU

COORDINATES
35.68854, 139.70066

WEBSITE
www.shinjuku-busterminal.co.jp

G

SHINJUKU GYOEN NATIONAL GARDEN

SHINJUKU

COORDINATES
35.68517, 139.71005

WEBSITE
www.env.go.jp

10

SUICA PENGUIN SQUARE

SHINJUKU

COORDINATES
35.68789, 139.70103

O

NTT DOCOMO YOYOGI TOWER

SHIBUYA

COORDINATES
35.6844, 139.70308

11

BIC CAMERA ELECTRONICS STORE

SHINJUKU

COORDINATES
35.69201, 139.70186

WEBSITE
www.biccamera.com

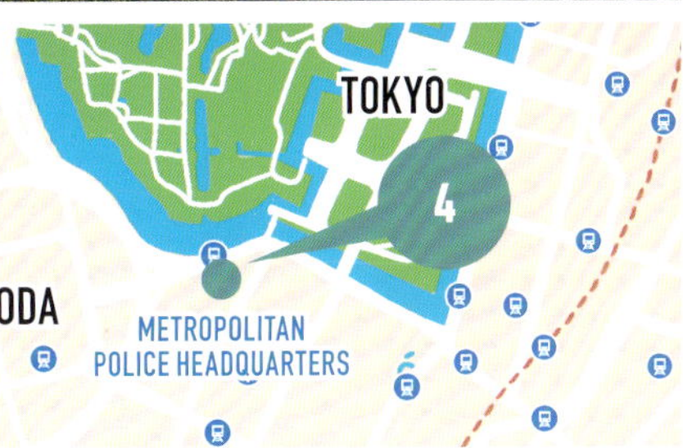

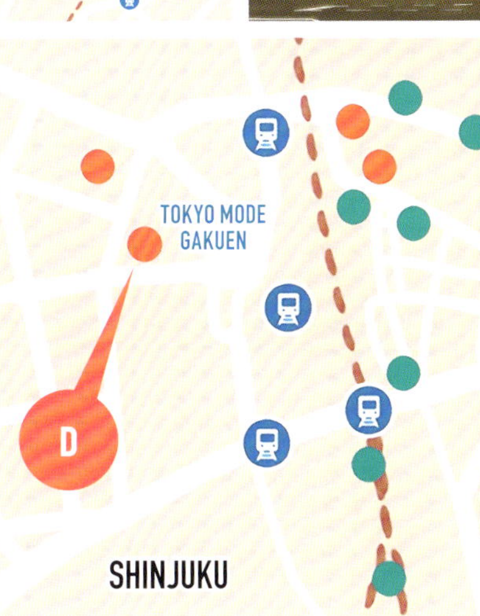

PUBLIC BUILDINGS

Some buildings (Tokyo Mode Gakuen, Tokyo Metropolitan Government Building, Sumitomo Building) are so iconic that they appear in numerous films set in Tokyo. And of course, it's only proper that the Metropolitan Police Headquarters in **Chiyoda** should feature both in a movie about a detective and in ***Death Note***.

DON QUIJOTE STORES

Laura drives her Mini into the heart of Kabukicho. She speeds past some Don Quijote stores and heads toward Toho Cinemas, where a statue of Godzilla's head (but no body) peeks out over the top of the building.

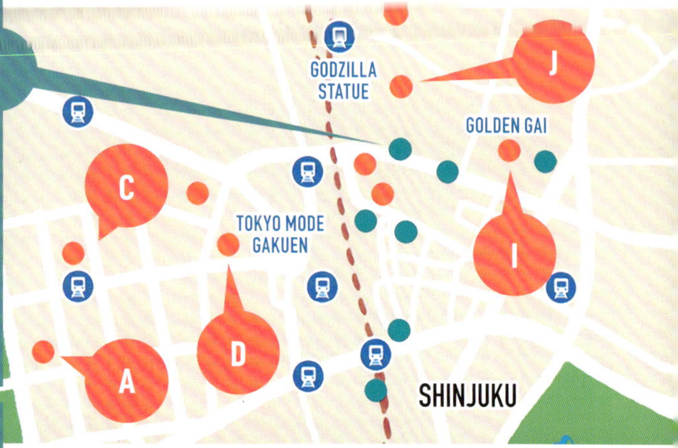

1

GODZILLA STATUE

GOLDEN GAI

TOKYO MODE GAKUEN

SHINJUKU

A

C

D

I

J

1

J
新宿
平成女学園
CAPSULE
PUB & BAR
AGEHA
2F
CURRY HOUSE
CoCo壱番屋
B1F
ダーツ
299円
麻雀
3F
最強の敵と、
最後の戦い。
9.8 FRI
ROADSHOW
〈宿命の対決〉始
MARUHAN
2F店舗出入口はビル左側
TOHO CINEMAS
カラオケ

JR SHINJUKU STATION, EAST ENTRANCE – LUMINE EST

Ai leans against a column in the **Lumine Est** underground shopping center waiting to be contacted by Ryo. A maze of packed shops really does exist beneath **JR Shinjuku Station**.

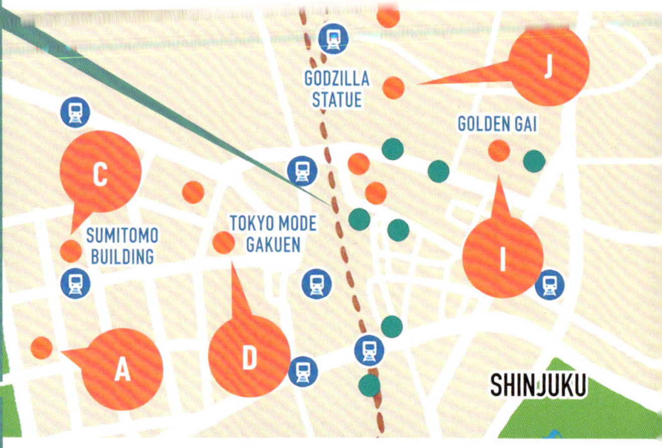

2

GODZILLA STATUE

GOLDEN GAI

SUMITOMO BUILDING

TOKYO MODE GAKUEN

SHINJUKU

2

JR SHINJUKU STATION, SOUTH ENTRANCE – SKYWAY

Ai, Ryo, and Kaori stand on the skyway that runs along the South Entrance to JR Shinjuku Station. Behind Ryo and Kaori is an escalator whose real-life counterpart can be seen on the right in the photo below.

3
JR SHINJUKU STATION
SHINJUKU
O
G
SHINJUKU GYOEN NATIONAL GARDEN
NTT DOCOMO YOYOGI TOWER

3

NEW YORK GRILL

Christopher and Laura dine at the New York Grill, a restaurant on the fifty-second floor of the **Park Hyatt Tokyo Hotel** with a breathtaking view of all of Shinjuku. The Tokyo Metropolitan Government Building and Tokyo Mode Gakuen stand out.

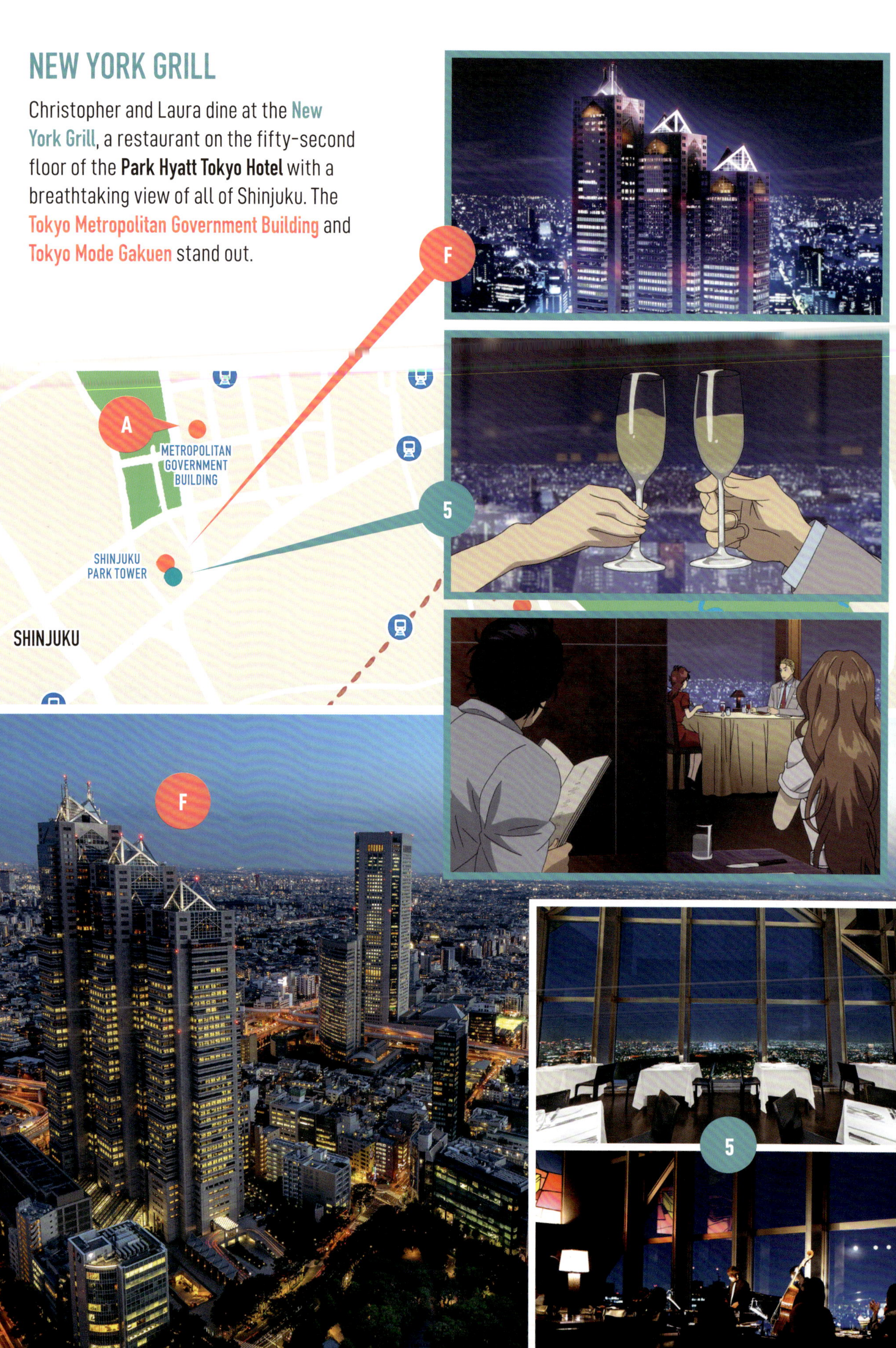

HANAZONO SHRINE

Ai is a model; to stay in shape, she exercises every morning by jogging to the Hanazono Shrine. Ryo follows her for her protection. The shrine is located near the Golden Gai district, a favorite spot for locals.

TOKYO BAY

Kaori is invited onto Shinji's yacht. In the background are some of the most famous landmarks of the manmade island of Odaiba, including the **Rainbow Bridge**, and, in the distance, the distinctive panoramic sphere of the **Fuji Television** skyscraper.

ISETAN DEPARTMENT STORE

In Shinjuku, Ai and Ryo stroll down a small street that runs alongside the **Isetan department store**. You'll want to stop by the fine foods section in the basement, where you'll find delicacies from all over the world—if you don't mind the cost!

SUBNADE

As Ryo and Ai are chased through the bowels of Shinjuku Station, they dart into the Subnade underground shopping center to evade their pursuers. From there, they take Exit 13 and emerge directly into the Kabukicho district near Golden Gai. An entire world lies beneath Shinjuku Station, just waiting to be explored.

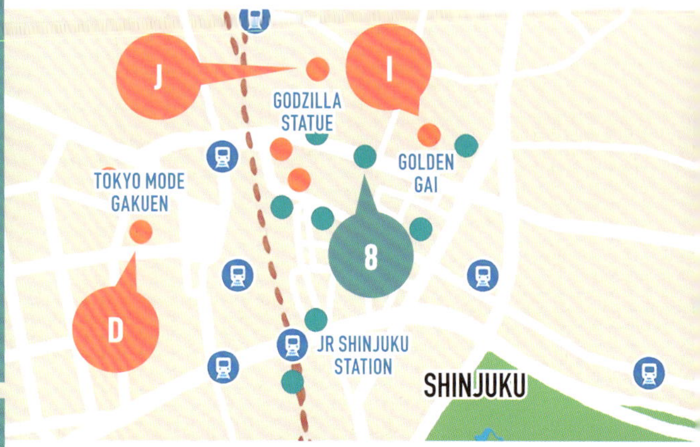

J
I
GODZILLA STATUE
GOLDEN GAI
TOKYO MODE GAKUEN
8
D
JR SHINJUKU STATION
SHINJUKU

GOLDEN GAI

The **Golden Gai** district is not only the ideal hiding place for Ryo and Ai, but it's also the perfect base from which to strike back at their pursuers, a paramilitary group under Shinji's command. Ryo entrusts Ai to an old innkeeper who runs one of the many tiny businesses stacked atop one another throughout the neighborhood.

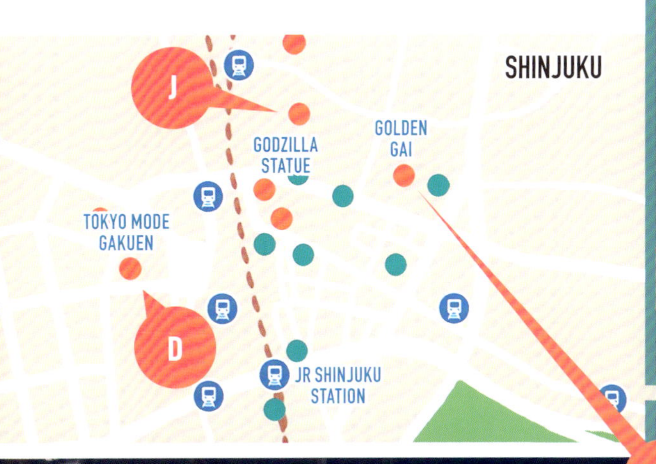

SHINJUKU PARK TOWER

After their ordeal in Golden Gai, Ryo takes Ai to a special place where he can show her the true heart of the city: the terrace at Shinjuku Park, which offers a panoramic view of the entire district.

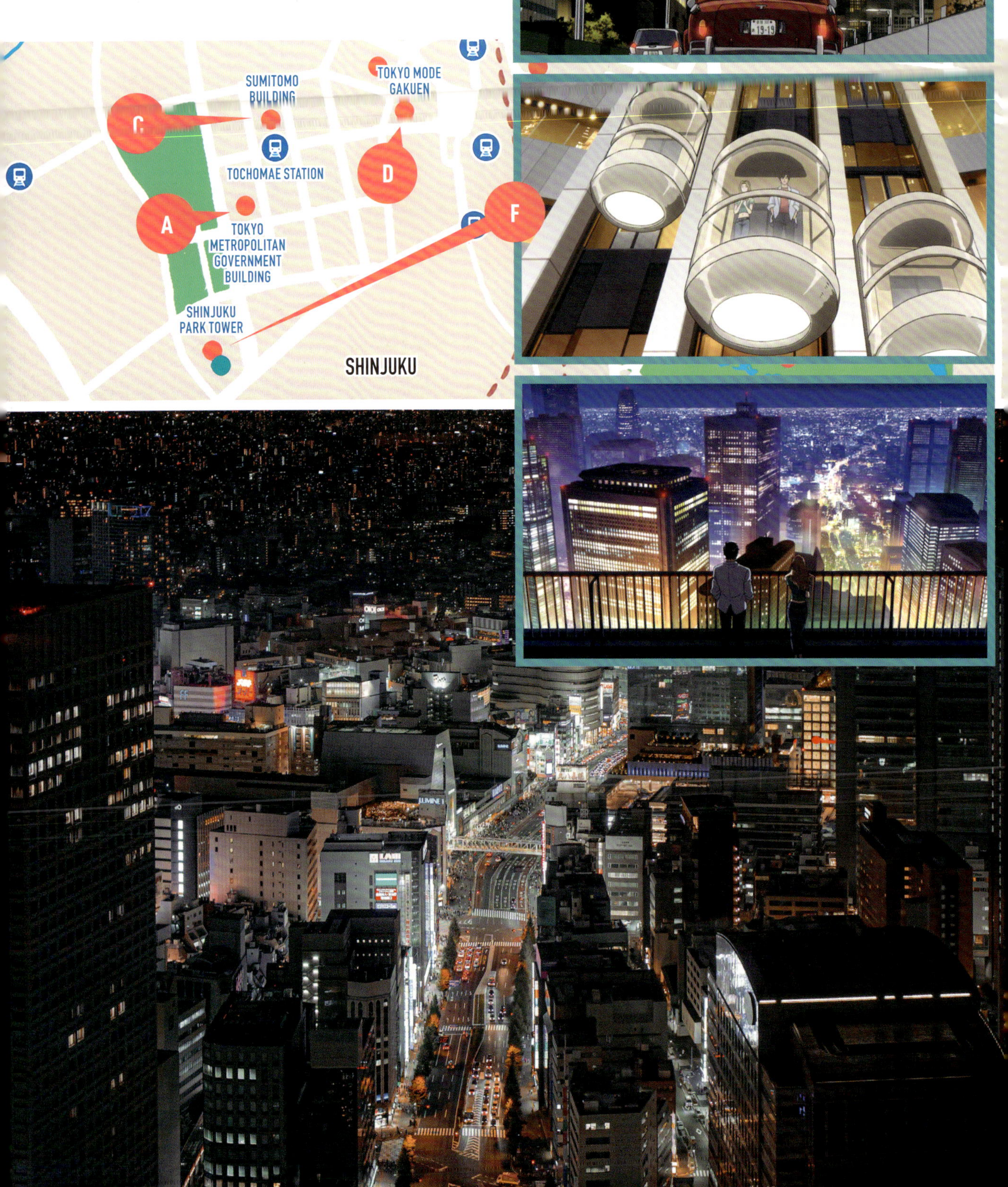

JR SHINJUKU STATION, SOUTH ENTRANCE

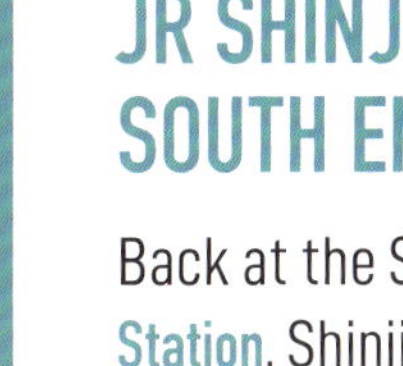

Back at the South Entrance of Shinjuku Station, Shinji's mercenaries abandon Ai after scanning her retina.

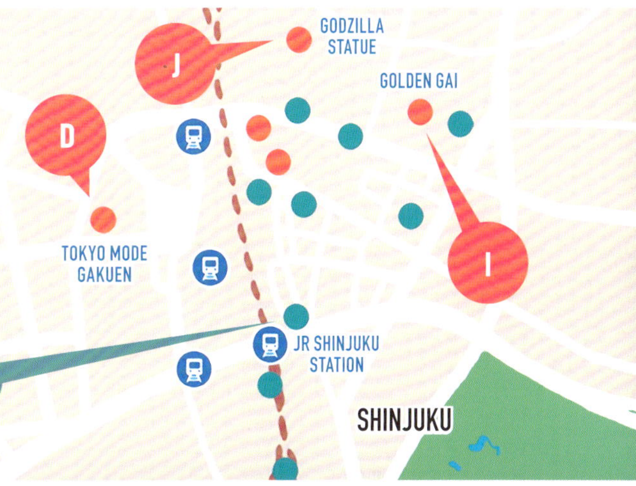

SHINJUKU BUS TERMINAL

When drones begin attacking JR Shinjuku Station, Ryo and Ai take refuge in the Shinjuku Bus Terminal, which connects to the station itself.

SHINJUKU GYOEN NATIONAL GARDEN

Ryo drives a bus to **Shinjuku Gyoen National Garden**. There, away from bystanders, he battles Shinji's drones and brings the story to an end.

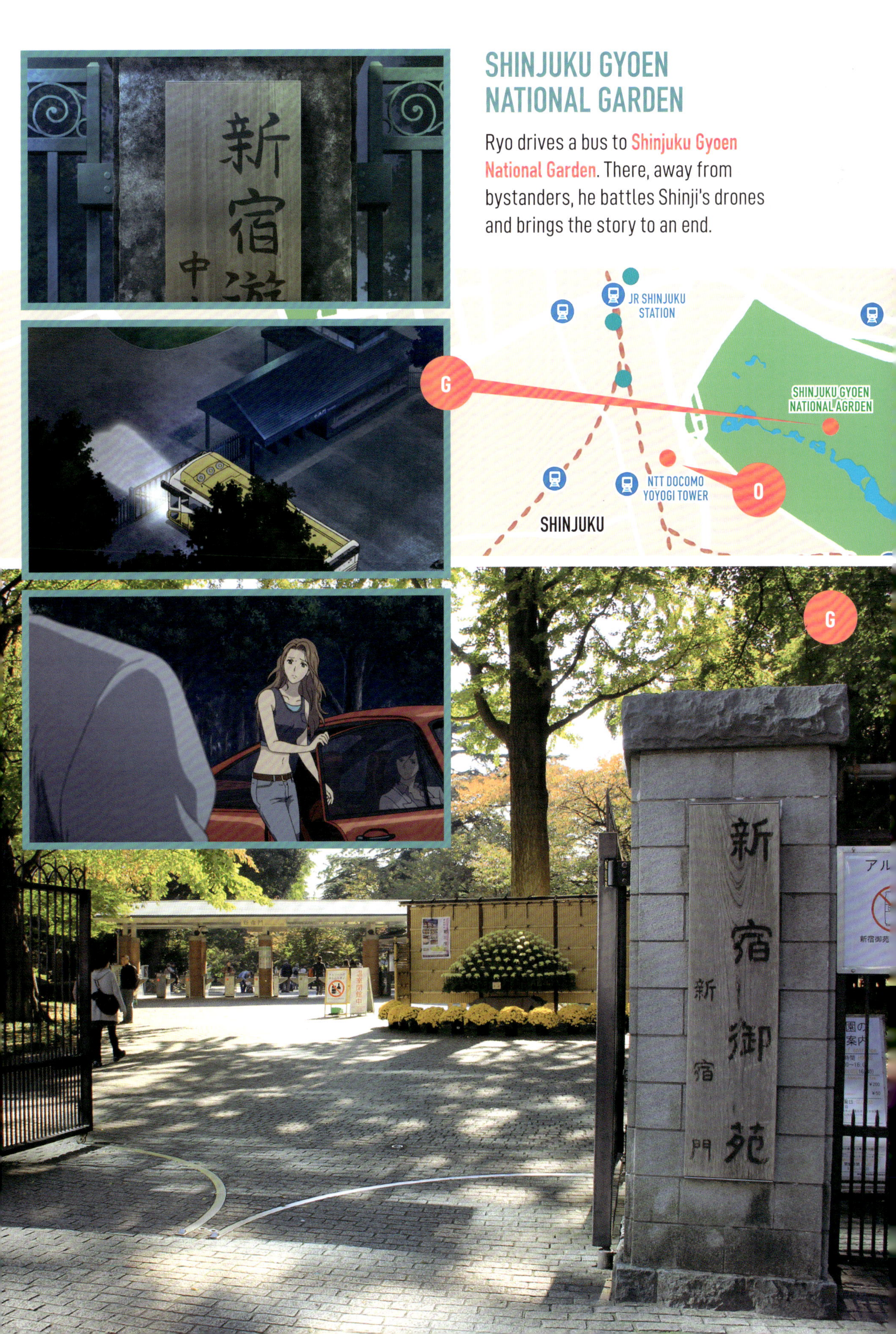

SHINJUKU GYOEN NATIONAL GARDEN

Umibozu joins the battle at Shinjuku Gyoen National Garden. He makes his escape by dashing over the garden's distinctive footbridge.

10

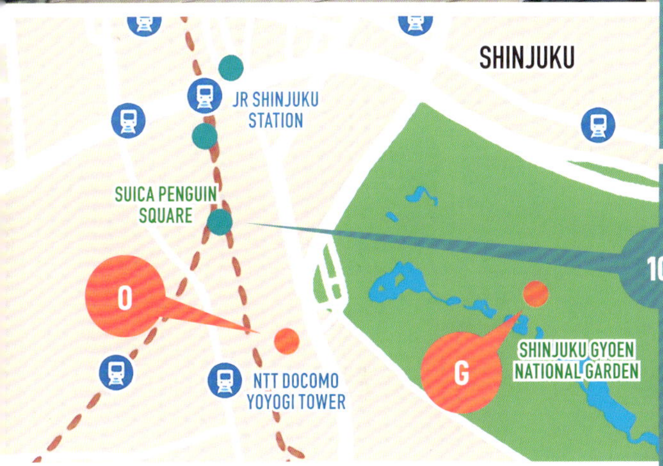

SHINJUKU

JR SHINJUKU STATION

SUICA PENGUIN SQUARE

O

10

G

SHINJUKU GYOEN NATIONAL GARDEN

NTT DOCOMO YOYOGI TOWER

SUICA PENGUIN SQUARE

On the panoramic terrace of Suica Penguin Square at JR Shinjuku Station, Kaori and Ryo bid farewell to Ai, who is determined to resume her medical studies. The plaza is worth a visit to see its lights at Christmastime. NTT Docomo Yoyogi Tower appears in the background of the final scene.

BIC CAMERA

After the credits, we see Kaori and Ryo again near JR Shinjuku Station. The iconic building that houses the Bic Camera electronics store appears behind them. It is seen often in the classic series and the manga, as is the chalkboard used to contact Ryo.

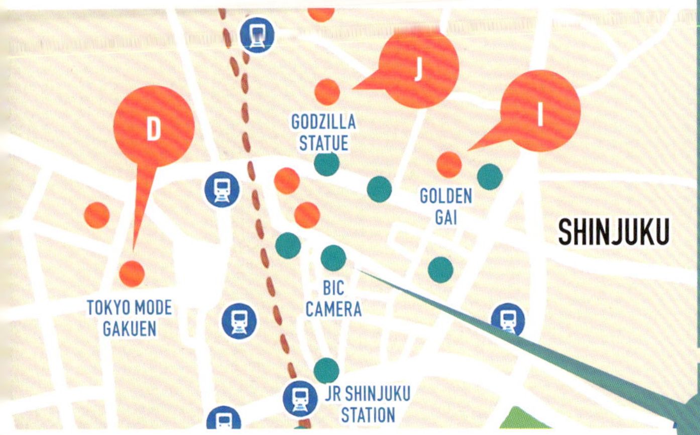

D
J
I
GODZILLA STATUE
GOLDEN GAI
SHINJUKU
TOKYO MODE GAKUEN
BIC CAMERA
JR SHINJUKU STATION
11

11

DEATH NOTE

Light Yagami is a top student who is living a boring life and suffering from deep depression. One day, Light stumbles upon a mysterious notebook called the *Death Note*, which was dropped into the human world by a *shinigami*, or god of death. The *Death Note* has an extraordinary power: If you know someone's face and write that person's name in the book, you can control when and how they die. Operating as a vigilante under the name Kira, Light uses the *Death Note* to "purify" the world and create a new order. However, his actions do not go unnoticed. They attract the attention of L, a brilliant private detective determined to uncover Kira's identity and stop him.

The chase between L and Kira mainly takes place in central Tokyo and West Tokyo. Light passes through **Shibuya Station** on his way home. His father works at the **Metropolitan Police Headquarters** in Chiyoda, in the heart of Tokyo. L installs the team tasked with uncovering Kira at the **Imperial Hotel** in the same district. Light also attends **Aoyama Gakuin University** in Minato ward.

DEATH NOTE

TETSURO ARAKI (2007)

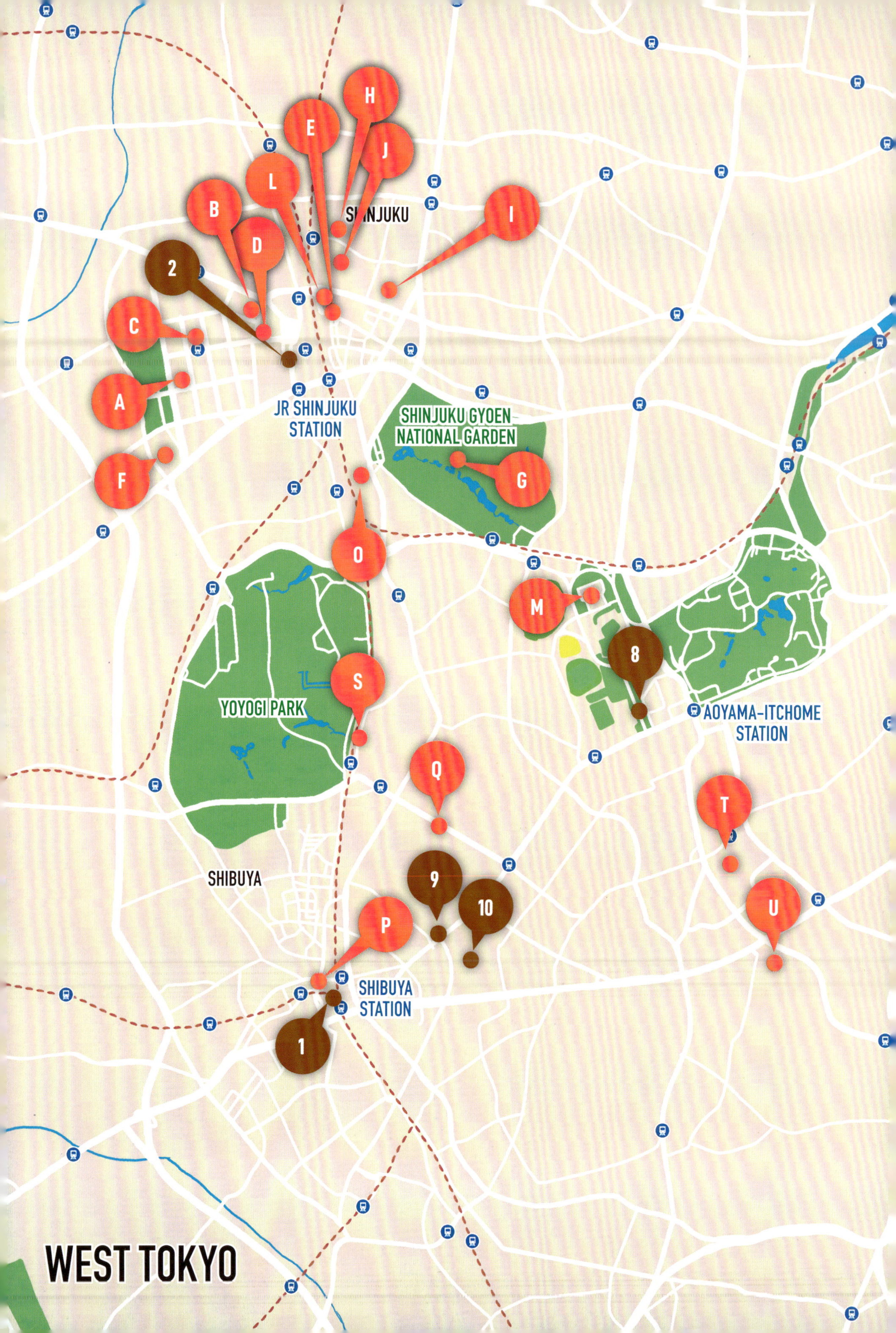

SHINJUKU
JR SHINJUKU STATION
SHINJUKU GYOEN NATIONAL GARDEN
YOYOGI PARK
AOYAMA-ITCHOME STATION
SHIBUYA
SHIBUYA STATION
A
B
C
D
E
F
G
H
I
J
L
M
O
P
Q
S
T
U
1
2
8
9
10
WEST TOKYO

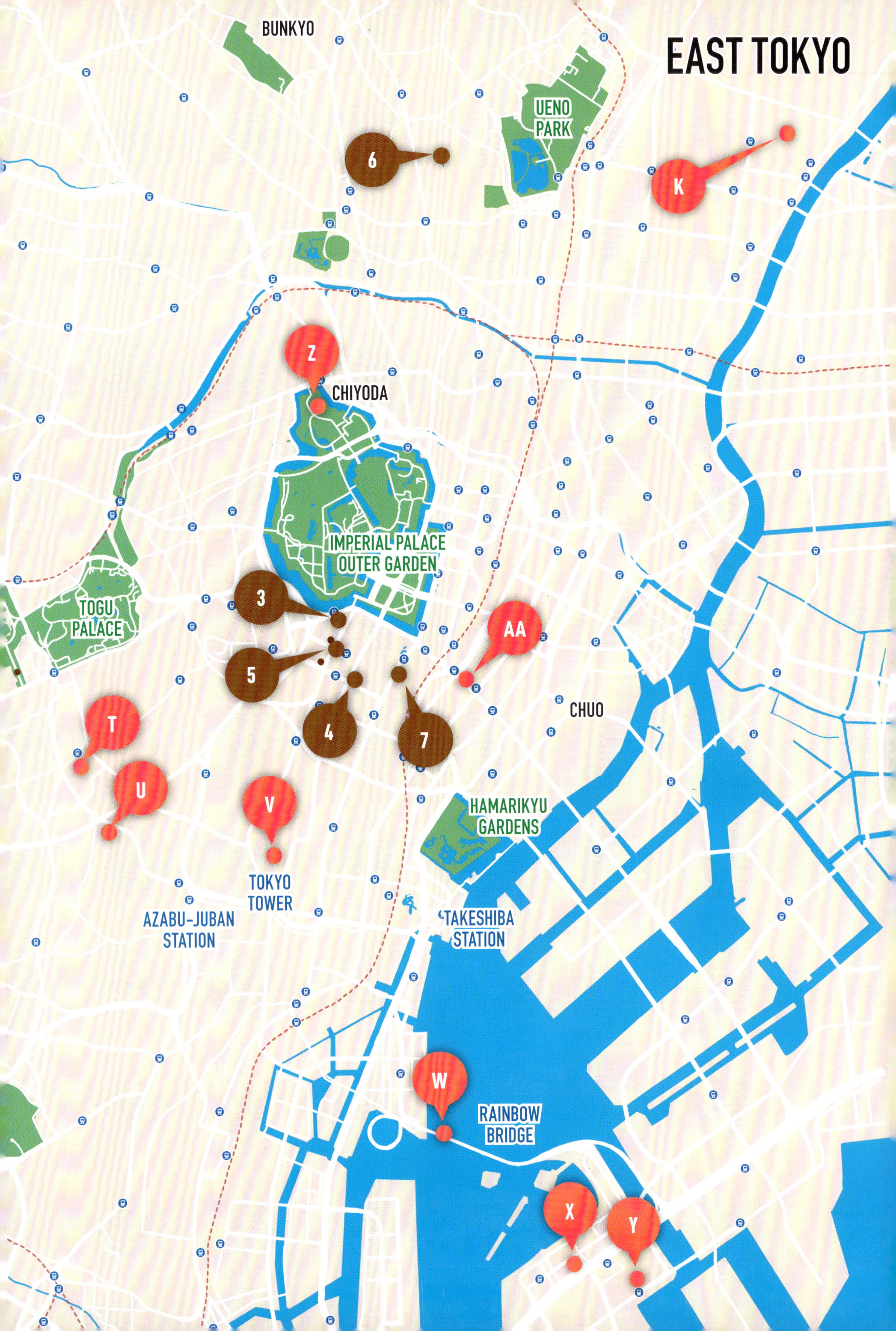
EAST TOKYO
BUNKYO
UENO PARK
6
K
Z
CHIYODA
IMPERIAL PALACE OUTER GARDEN
TOGU PALACE
3
5
4
7
AA
CHUO
T
U
V
TOKYO TOWER
AZABU-JUBAN STATION
HAMARIKYU GARDENS
TAKESHIBA STATION
W
RAINBOW BRIDGE
X
Y

1

JR SHIBUYA STATION

SHIBUYA

COORDINATES
35.65803, 139.70163

P

SHIBUYA INTERSECTION

SHIBUYA

COORDINATES
35.65948, 139.70055

2

ODAKYU ACE

SHINJUKU

COORDINATES
35.69023, 139.6986

WEBSITE
www.odakyu-ace.jp

3

METROPOLITAN POLICE HEADQUARTERS

CHIYODA

COORDINATES
35.67669, 139.75203

4

SEAGULL FOUNTAIN

CHIYODA

COORDINATES
35.67223, 139.75344

WEBSITE
www.tokyo-park.or.jp

5

KASUMIGASEKI STATION

CHIYODA

COORDINATES
35.67425,139.75115

Z

NIPPON BUDOKAN

CHIYODA

COORDINATES
35.69333, 139.7497

WEBSITE
www.nipponbudokan.or.jp

6 IMPERIAL UNIVERSITY OF TOKYO

BUNKYO

COORDINATES
35.71267, 139.76198

WEBSITE
www.u-tokyo.ac.jp

7 IMPERIAL HOTEL TOKYO

CHIYODA

COORDINATES
35.67245, 139.7579

WEBSITE
www.imperialhotel.co.jp

E STUDIO ALTA (SHINJUKU DAIBIRU)

SHINJUKU

COORDINATES
35.69272, 139.7013

Y PANORAMIC ROAD

KOTO

COORDINATES
35.62635, 139.78223

W RAINBOW BRIDGE

MINATO

COORDINATES
35.63656, 139.76314

V TOKYO TOWER

MINATO

COORDINATES
35.65858, 139.74543

WEBSITE
www.tokyotower.co.jp

S TAKESHITA DORI

SHIBUYA

COORDINATES
35.67103, 139.70517

8

MEIJI SHRINE GARDEN

MINATO

COORDINATES
35.67271, 139.72057

WEBSITE
www.meijijingugaien.jp

9

KODOMO NO KI (TREE OF CHILDREN) SCULPTURE

SHIBUYA

COORDINATES
35.66177, 139.70799

10

AOYAMA GAKUIN UNIVERSITY

SHIBUYA

COORDINATES
35.66051, 139.70996

WEBSITE
www.aoyama.ac.jp

JR SHIBUYA STATION

EPISODE 1

Like the thousands of people who rush through Shibuya every day, Light passes through JR Shibuya Station and the iconic intersection outside it on his way home from high school.

ODAKYU ACE, LOTTERIA & SABOTEN

EPISODE 5

Light waits for FBI agent Raye Penber in the underground corridors of Shinjuku Station, inside the **South Building of the Odakyu Ace** underground shopping center, which connects directly to **Shinjuku Station**.

Restaurants and shops line the underground passageways. Light and his *shinigami* lean against the entrance of **Saboten**, a small restaurant offering takeout and specializing in *tonkatsu*, the traditional Japanese breaded pork cutlet. In another scene is a sign for the popular Japanese fast food chain **Lotteria**. Both signs are altered in the show.

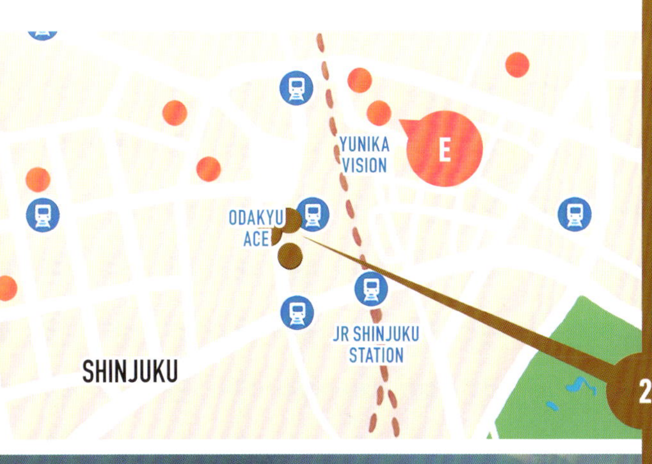

YAMANOTE LINE

EPISODE 5

The JR Yamanote line stops at **Shinjuku Station**. After his conversation with Light, Agent Penber waits for his train on Platform 12.

NAOMI AND LIGHT'S STROLL

EPISODE 6

Naomi and Light chat while strolling through the streets around the government buildings in Chiyoda. Their route starts at the **Metropolitan Police Headquarters (3)**, crosses the intersection outside the corner of the **Ministry of Internal Affairs (B) (35.67552, 139.75127)**, and continues straight to the intersection **(C)** outside the **Ministry of Foreign Affairs (35.67418, 139.74994)**. Here, they cross the street and turn right toward **Seagull Fountain** in **Hibiya Park (4)**.

SEAGULL FOUNTAIN HIBIYA PARK

EPISODES 6 & 7

Naomi and Light end up at **Seagull Fountain** in **Hibiya Park**. They stop briefly to chat next to the fountain and then head back the way they came.

KASUMIGASEKI METRO STATION

EPISODES 6 & 7

On the way back, Naomi and Light pass near the entrance to the **Kasumigaseki metro station (5)**. After exchanging a few words, they head back toward the **Metropolitan Police Headquarters (3)**, where they started, and then part ways.

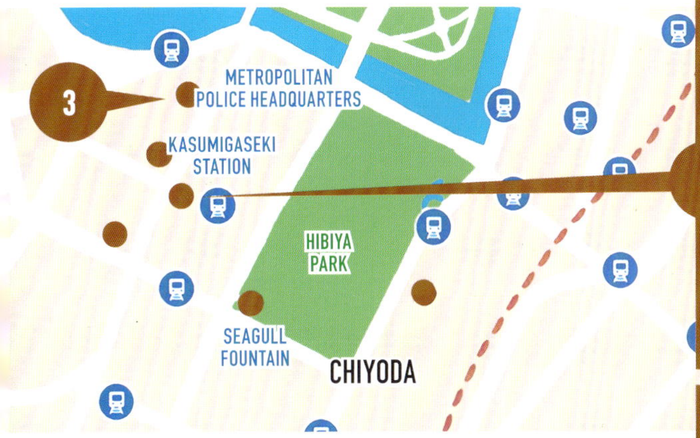

3 METROPOLITAN POLICE HEADQUARTERS

KASUMIGASEKI STATION

5

HIBIYA PARK

SEAGULL FOUNTAIN

CHIYODA

5

NIPPON BUDOKAN

EPISODE 9

Light and L's graduation ceremony is held at **Nippon Budokan** arena, a multipurpose event center big enough to hold entire graduating classes.

KUDANSHITA STATION

CHIYODA

NIPPON BUDOKAN

KITANOMARU PARK

TAKEBASHI STATION

Z

Z

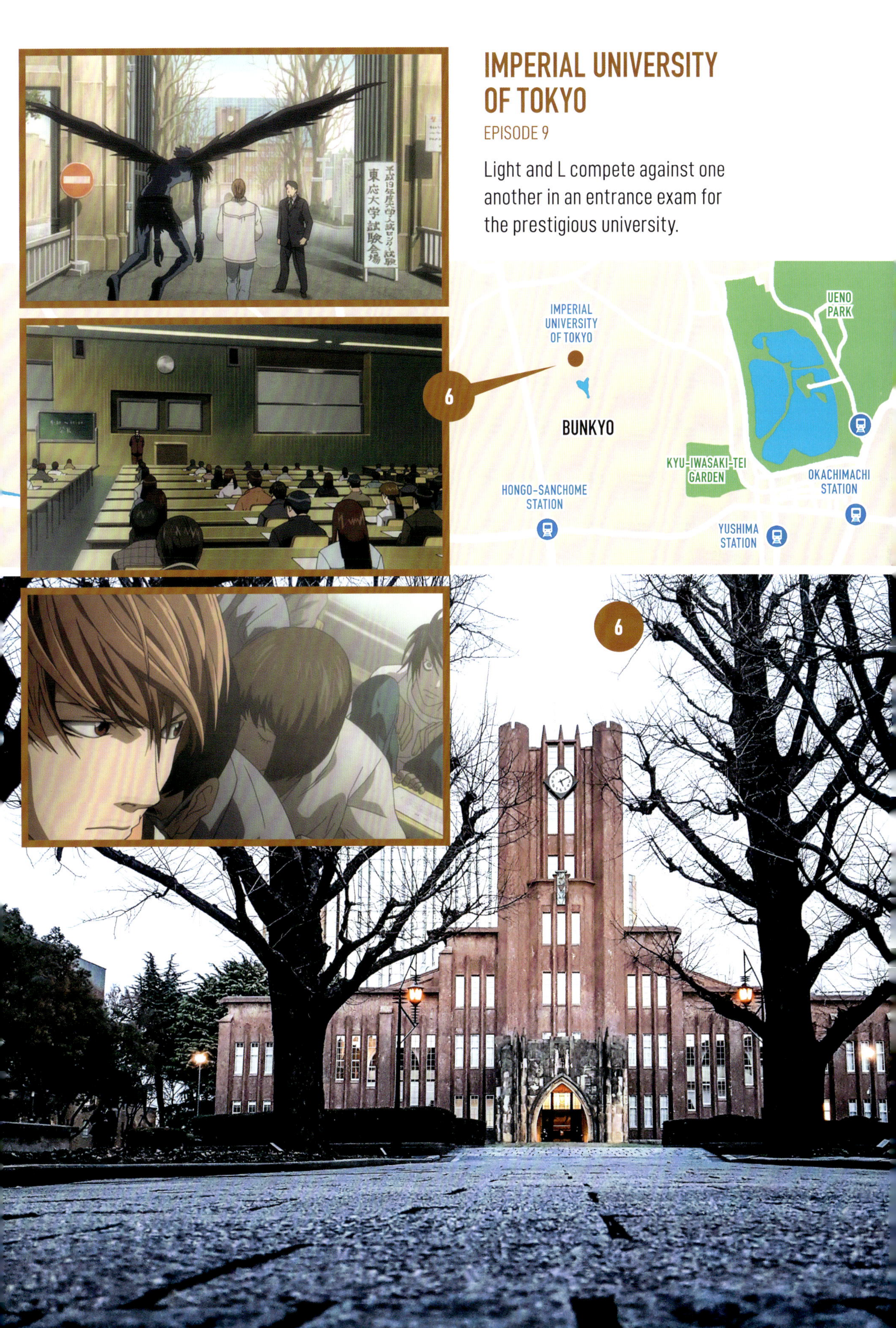

IMPERIAL UNIVERSITY OF TOKYO

EPISODE 9

Light and L compete against one another in an entrance exam for the prestigious university.

IMPERIAL HOTEL TOKYO

EPISODE 9

L sets up his headquarters at this luxurious hotel overlooking **Hibiya Park**.

STUDIO ALTA (SHINJUKU DAIBIRU)

EPISODE 11

Kira's message to the Japanese people is broadcast on the big screen at **Studio Alta** in Shinjuku. The people of Tokyo listen while images of the city's iconic landmarks flash by.

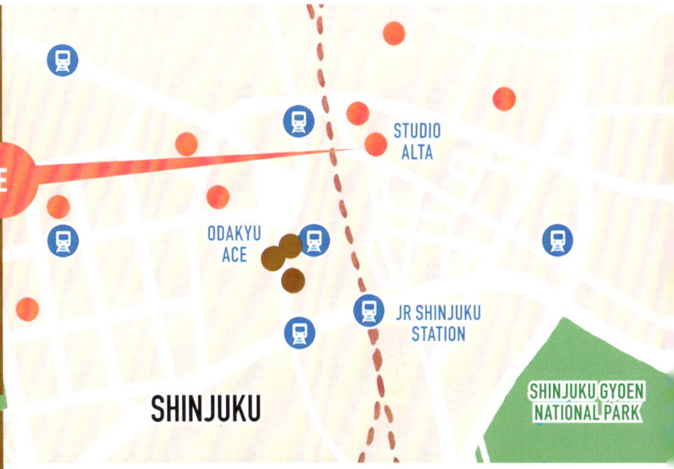

STUDIO ALTA
ODAKYU ACE
JR SHINJUKU STATION
SHINJUKU
SHINJUKU GYOEN NATIONAL PARK

RAINBOW BRIDGE & DAIKANRANSHA FERRIS WHEEL

EPISODE 11

As Kira continues to broadcast his message, his voice echoes across images of the **Rainbow Bridge** and the **Daikanransha Ferris wheel** located on the artificial island of Odaiba.

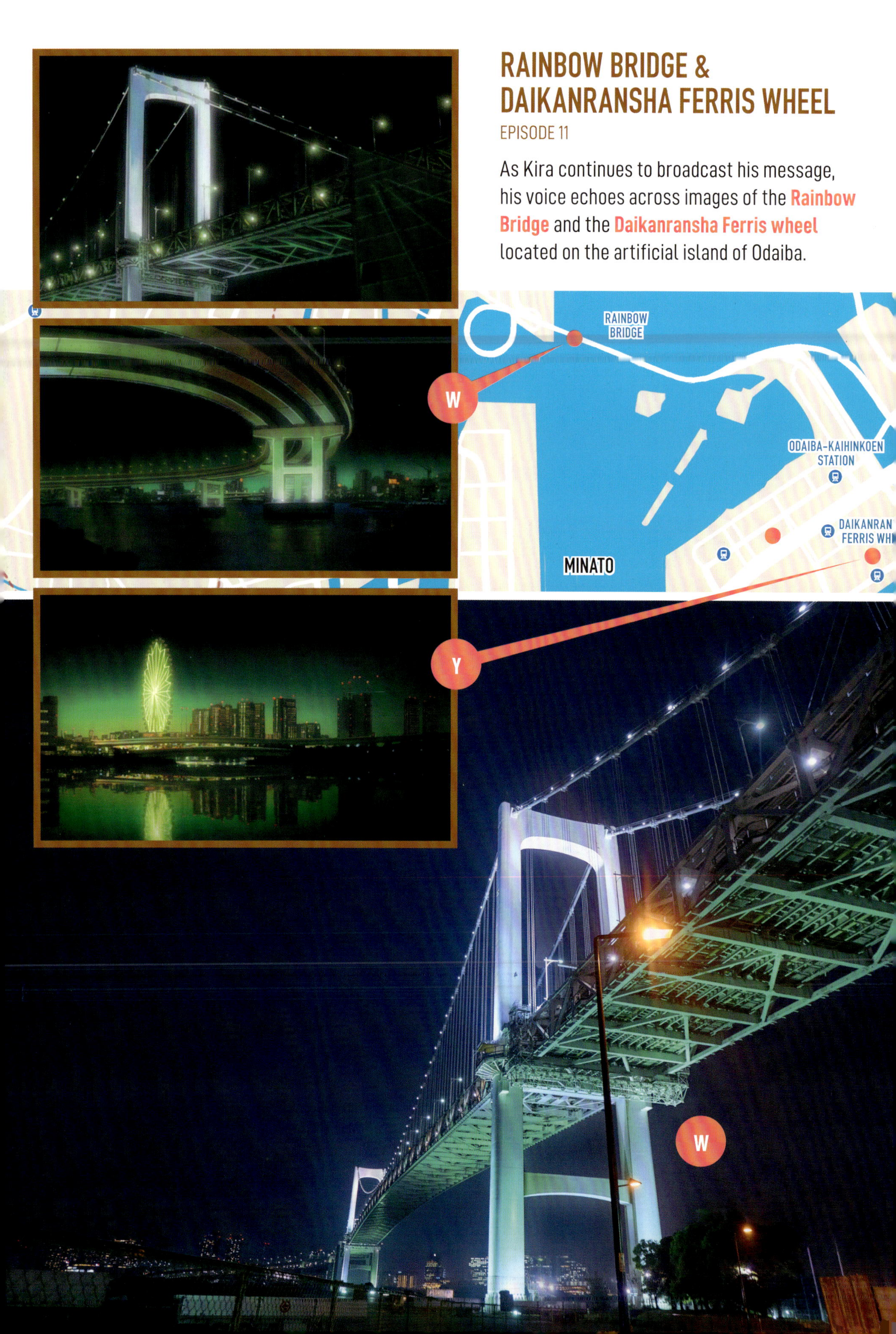

TOKYO TOWER

EPISODE 11

The images of Odaiba are followed by ones of **Tokyo Tower** and the highway to Shibuya.

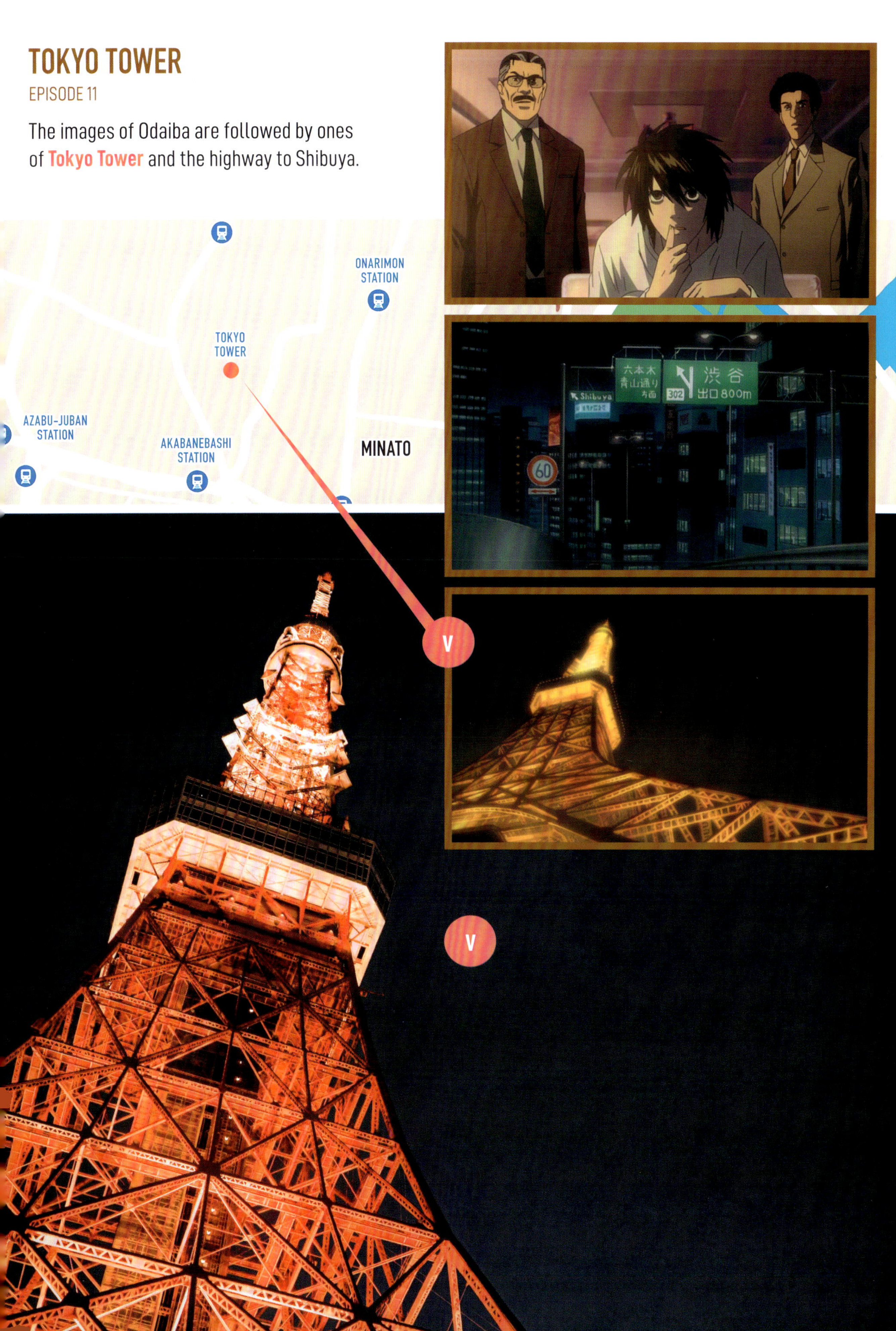

TAKESHITA STREET

EPISODE 11

We watch Misa walk down **Takeshita Dori**, the most well-known commercial street in Harajuku.

MEIJI JINGU GAIEN

EPISODE 13

This tree-lined avenue connects the **Meiji Jingu Museum** gardens to **Aoyama Street**. The **Kodomo no Ki** ("Tree of Children") sculpture is located farther down the same street, toward Shibuya Station.

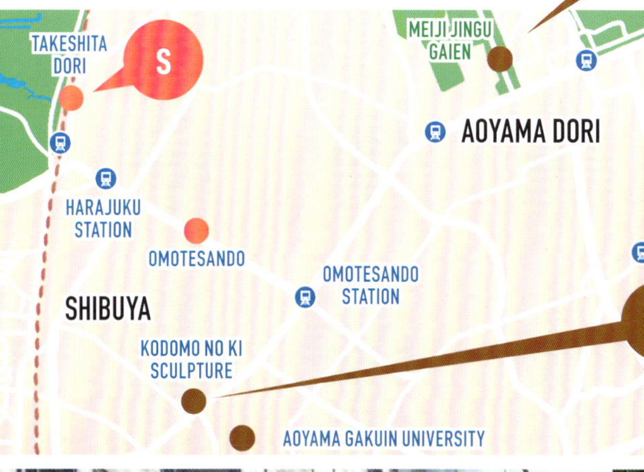

AOYAMA GAKUIN UNIVERSITY

EPISODE 15

Light and L are on the university campus, where Misa joins them shortly afterward.

SAILOR MOON

Usagi Tsukino is a lively fourteen-year-old girl and a clumsy crybaby. Her life takes an unexpected turn when she meets Luna, a black cat with a crescent moon on her forehead. Luna gives her a magical brooch that allows her to transform into Sailor Moon, a beautiful warrior of love and justice. Usagi and the other Sailor Guardians are tasked with finding the mysterious, legendary Silver Crystal and protecting Princess Serenity of the Moon Kingdom. Unfortunately, the evil Queen Beryl of the Dark Kingdom sends her loyal servants to Tokyo to seize the powerful crystal.

Pretty Guardian Sailor Moon Crystal was produced by Toei Animation to commemorate the twentieth anniversary of the classic series and was intended to be a faithful adaptation of Naoko Takeuchi's original manga.

Like Takeuchi herself, the Sailor Guardians all live in or near the Azabu-Juban district of Minato, a bustling residential area in central Tokyo that is home to a wide variety of shops, restaurants, and bars. Its central location and proximity to Hiroo and Roppongi make it one of the trendiest and most sought-after residential areas in Tokyo. The center feels like a small village, with narrow streets, slow traffic, and shops that have been run by the same owners for years.

SAILOR MOON

JUNICHI SATO (1992)
SAILOR MOON **- 46 EPISODES**

MUNEHISA SAKAI (2014)
SAILOR MOON CRYSTAL **- 39 EPISODES**

CHIAKI KON (2021)
SAILOR MOON ETERNAL **- FILM**

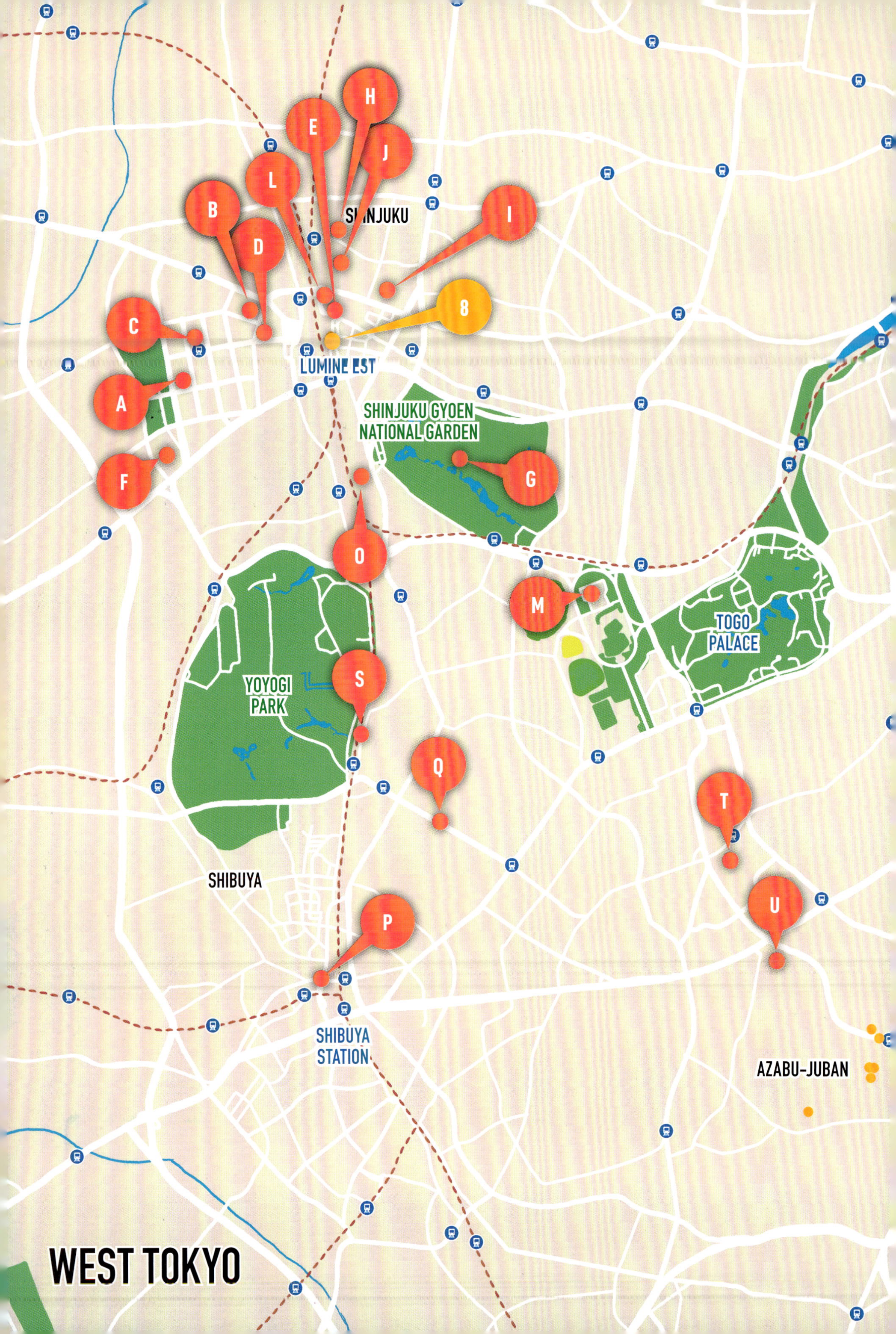
SHINJUKU
LUMINE EST
SHINJUKU GYOEN NATIONAL GARDEN
YOYOGI PARK
TOGO PALACE
SHIBUYA
SHIBUYA STATION
AZABU-JUBAN
A
B
C
D
E
F
G
H
I
J
L
M
O
P
Q
S
T
U
8
WEST TOKYO

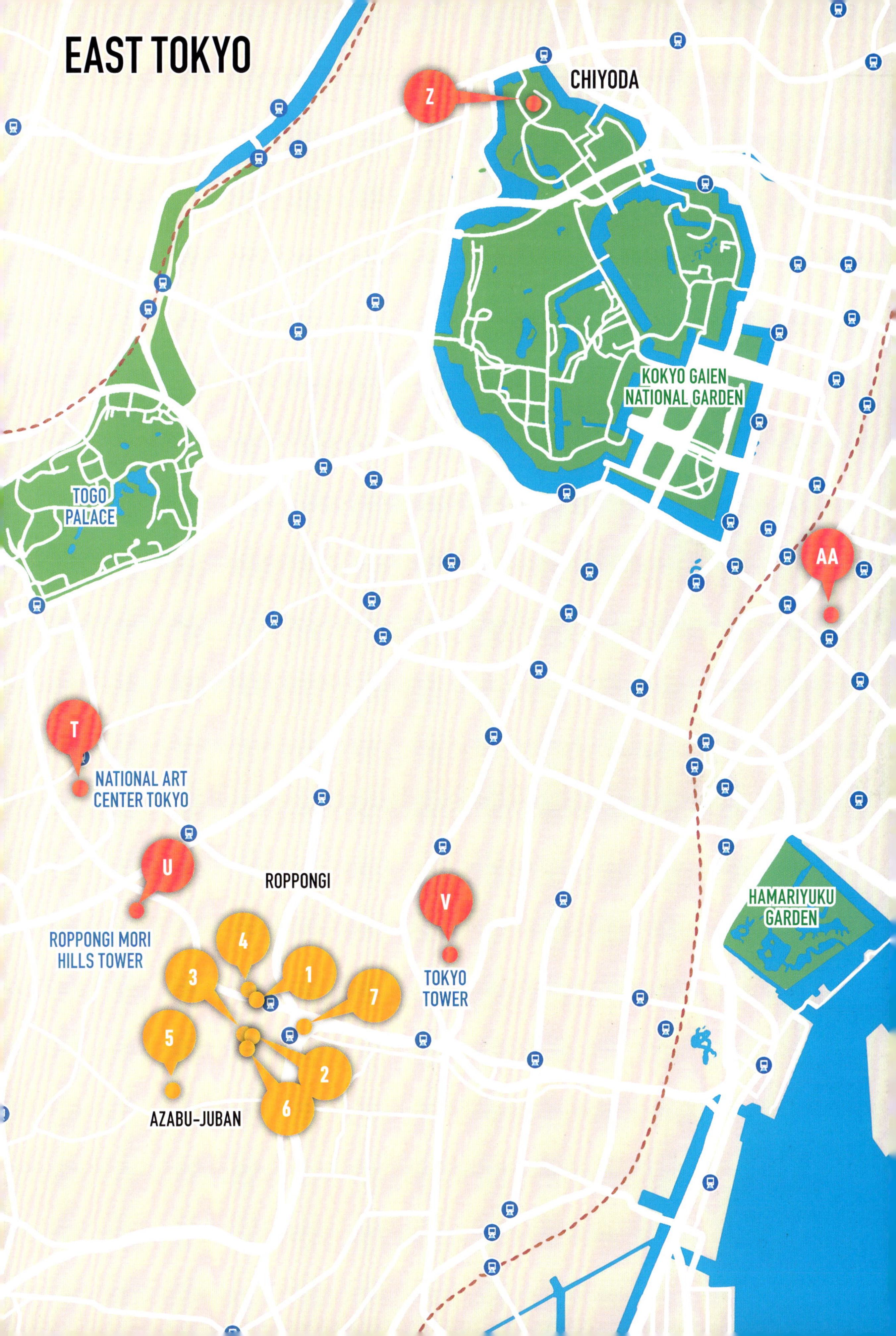
EAST TOKYO
Z
CHIYODA
KOKYO GAIEN
NATIONAL GARDEN
TOGO
PALACE
AA
T
NATIONAL ART
CENTER TOKYO
U
ROPPONGI
V
ROPPONGI MORI
HILLS TOWER
4
3
1
7
TOKYO
TOWER
5
2
6
AZABU-JUBAN
HAMARIYUKU
GARDEN

1

AZABU-JUBAN STATION

MINATO

COORDINATES
35.65639, 139.7366

2

PATIO JUBAN

MINATO

COORDINATES
35.65517, 139.73512

WEBSITE
www.visit-minato-city.tokyo

3

KIMI-CHAN STATUE

MINATO

COORDINATES
35.65517, 139.73499

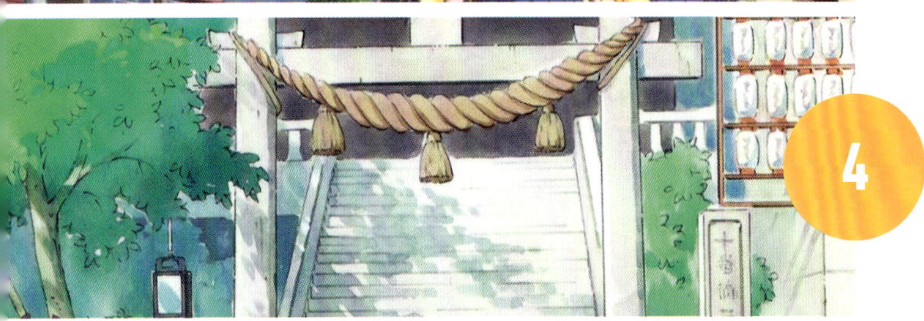

4

JUBAN INARI-JINJA SHRINE

MINATO

COORDINATES
35.65701, 139.73507

WEBSITE
www.jubaninari.or.jp

5

AZABU HIKAWA SHRINE

MINATO

COORDINATES
35.65289, 139.73104

WEBSITE
www.azabuhikawa.or.jp

V

TOKYO TOWER

MINATO

COORDINATES
35.65858, 139.74543

WEBSITE
www.tokyotower.co.jp

6

KALEIDOSCOPE MUKASHI-KAN

MINATO

COORDINATES
35.65459, 139.735

WEBSITE
www.brewster.co.jp

7 ICHINOHASHI PARK

MINATO

COORDINATES
35.6558, 139.73763

E STUDIO ALTA (SHINJUKU DAIBIRU)

SHINJUKU

COORDINATES
35.69272, 139.7013

AA GINZA WAKO

CHUO

COORDINATES
35.67173, 139.76504

S TAKESHITA STREET

SHIBUYA

COORDINATES
35.67103, 139.70517

8 LUMINE EST

SHINJUKU

COORDINATES
35.69125, 139.70114

WEBSITE
www.lumine.ne.jp

AZABU-JUBAN METRO STATION

SAILOR MOON CRYSTAL - EPISODE 2

Azabu-Juban is a quiet district in the heart of Minato. Its commercial streets are full of shops that have been around for years, and it is also home to several embassies. Rumor has it that this is where Naoko Takeuchi, author of ***Sailor Moon***, lives.

PATIO JUBAN

SAILOR MOON CRYSTAL - EPISODES 2 & 3

Patio Juban is a small, multipurpose pedestrian plaza that often hosts city-organized events. The surrounding trees offer some respite on sunny afternoons.

KIMI-CHAN STATUE

SAILOR MOON CRYSTAL - EPISODES 2 & 3

The famous 1921 Japanese song *The Red Shoes* was inspired by a little girl named Kimi Iwasaki, whose family entrusted her to an American missionary who was supposed to take her abroad. However, she fell seriously ill with tuberculosis and never left Japan. Instead, she was abandoned in an orphanage, now the **Juban Inari-jinja Shrine**, where she died in 1911 at the age of nine. The statue erected in her honor is a symbol of hope and resilience for its visitors. The third image down is from the original ***Sailor Moon*** series. The statue appears in several episodes.

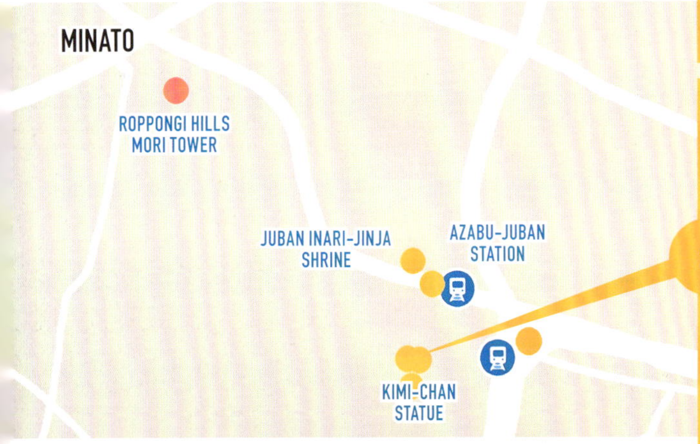

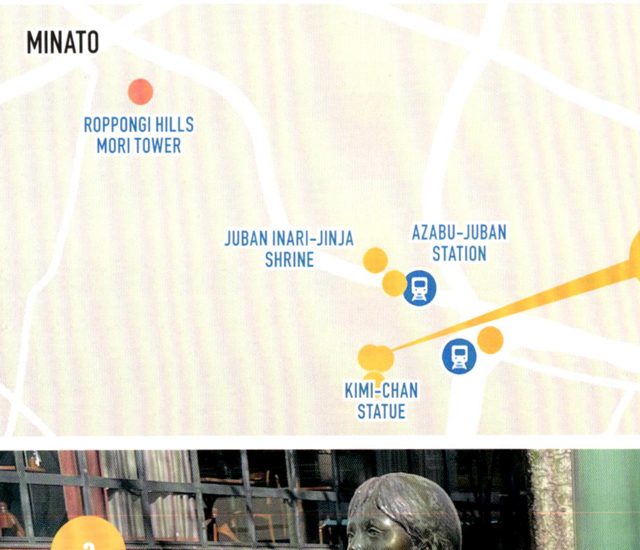

JUBAN INARI-JINJA SHRINE

SAILOR MOON CRYSTAL - EPISODE 3

The **Suehiro** and **Takecho Inari** shrines merged to form the Juban Inari-jinja Shrine, famous as the home of an amulet that protects against fire.

AZABU HIKAWA SHRINE

SAILOR MOON CRYSTAL – EPISODES 5 & 14

In a small shrine atop a hill, Rei Hino (Sailor Mars) serves as a priestess. Today, the shrine is a popular pilgrimage site for fans of the series—so much so that *ema* (small wooden plaques for writing prayers) featuring the characters have been specially created.

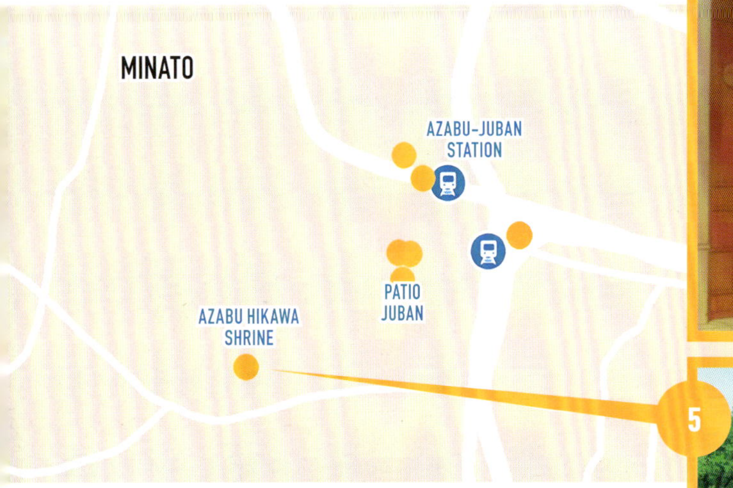

MINATO

AZABU-JUBAN STATION

PATIO JUBAN

AZABU HIKAWA SHRINE

5

5

TOKYO TOWER

SAILOR MOON CRYSTAL - EPISODE 9

Tokyo Tower appears frequently throughout the various ***Sailor Moon*** films and series. In ***Sailor Moon Crystal***, it can be seen from Mamoru's bedroom window. It also serves as the backdrop for a battle.

KALEIDOSCOPE MUKASHI-KAN

SAILOR MOON ETERNAL

This boutique of fine collectibles is worth a visit, if only to admire the myriad items on display. The shop is most famous for its kaleidoscopes adorned with colorful semiprecious stones.

6

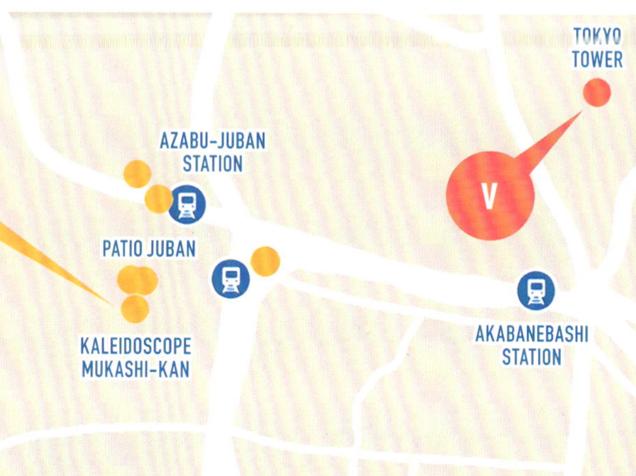

MINATO

6

ICHINOHASHI PARK

SAILOR MOON ETERNAL

This recently renovated public park runs alongside a waterway and under elevated roadways. This location is important to the Sailor Guardians, and it also appears in the original series.

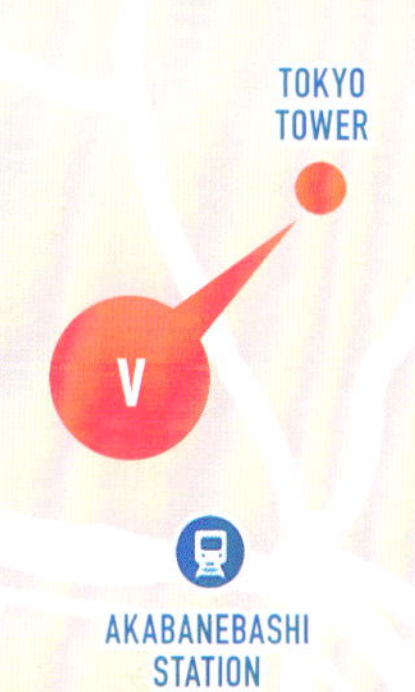

STUDIO ALTA (SHINJUKU DAIBIRU)

SAILOR MOON S: THE MOVIE

In the opening of the movie, Usagi, Chibiusa, and the other Sailor Guardians appear in front of the **Studio Alta** building in Shinjuku. The battle then moves to Ginza, where the **Ginza Wako** building can be seen amid the ice.

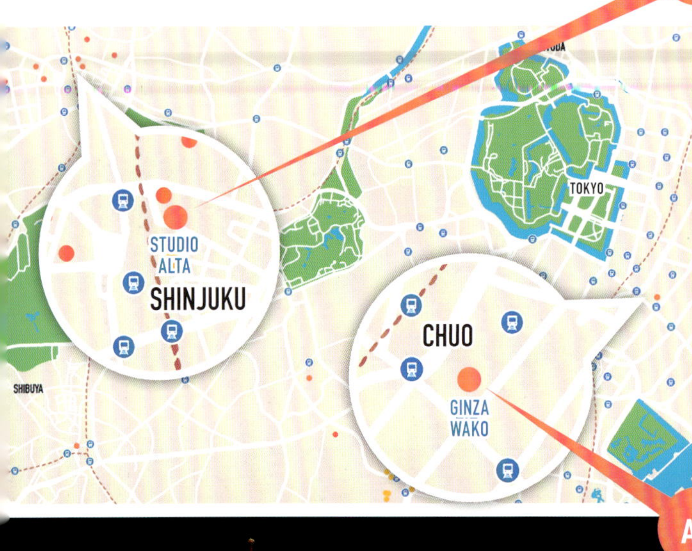

TAKESHITA DORI

SAILOR MOON - EPISODE 9

Takeshita Dori in Harajuku is a can't-miss destination for affordable shopping. Just a few blocks away, on the parallel street Omotesando, you'll find name-brand fashion boutiques.

LUMINE EST (FORMERLY MY CITY)

SAILOR MOON - EPISODE 19

Located in the same building as **JR Shinjuku Station**, Lumine Est was once known as **My City** shopping center.

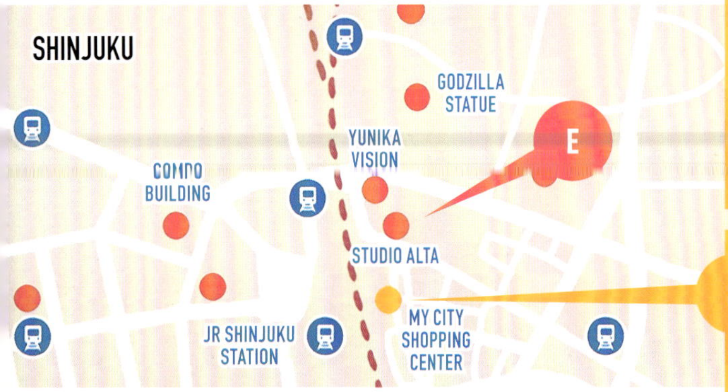

MY NEIGHBOR TOTORO

HAYAO MIYAZAKI (1988)

MY NEIGHBOR TOTORO

The story is set in the suburbs of Tokyo in the 1950s. Two young sisters, Satsuki and Mei, move with their father to Tokorozawa, a small rural village, to be closer to their mother, who is hospitalized there. While moving in, Satsuki and Mei encounter mysterious little creatures called soot sprites (*makkuro kurosuke*), which live in old, abandoned houses and can be seen only by children.

While exploring their new home, Mei also meets two curious long-eared creatures. She follows them to a large camphor tree, where she meets Totoro, a friendly forest spirit. Mei's father and sister are skeptical at first and aren't surprised when they can't find this Totoro. However, hoping to appease Mei, the father spins a story, explaining that Totoro is the guardian of the forest and that meeting him is a privilege reserved for the lucky few.

Totoro makes another appearance one rainy evening when Satsuki and Mei await their father at the bus stop. A few days later, Mei receives a call from the hospital. Worried about her mother's health, Mei tries to go to her but gets lost. A desperate Satsuki asks Totoro for help. He summons the Catbus to take her to Mei. Together, they manage to reach the hospital, and the two girls are reunited with their mother.

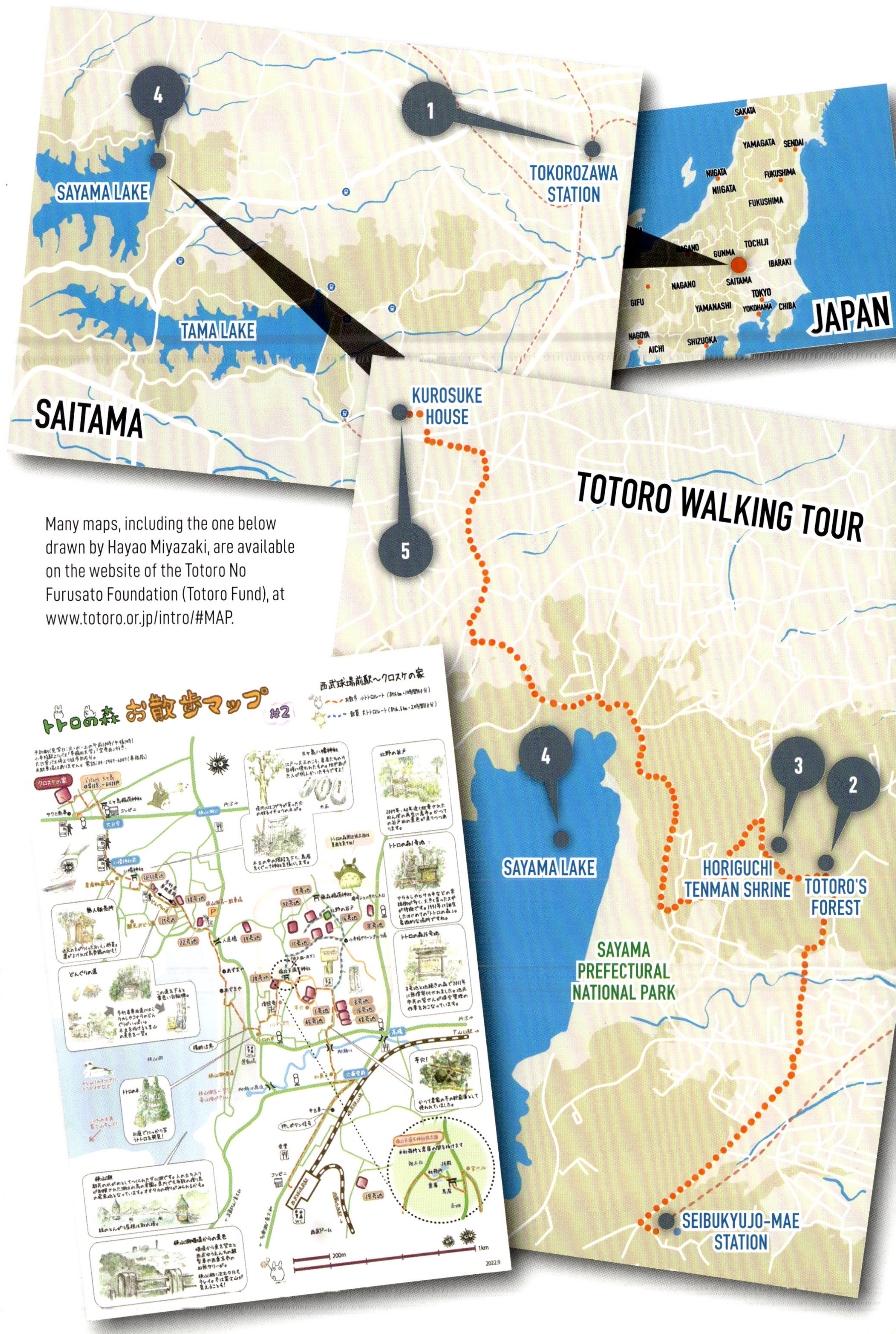

Many maps, including the one below drawn by Hayao Miyazaki, are available on the website of the Totoro No Furusato Foundation (Totoro Fund), at www.totoro.or.jp/intro/#MAP.

1

TOTORO STATUE

SAITAMA PREFECTURE

COORDINATES

35.78667, 139.47482

WEBSITE

www.city.tokorozawa.saitama.jp

2

TOTORO'S FOREST

SAITAMA PREFECTURE

COORDINATES

35.78018, 139.42185

WEBSITE

www.totoro.or.jp

3

HORIGUCHI TENMAN SHRINE

SAITAMA PREFECTURE

COORDINATES

35.78104, 139.42

WEBSITE

www.saitama-jinjacho.or.jp

4

SAYAMA LAKE

SAITAMA PREFECTURE

COORDINATES

35.77643, 139.40536

WEBSITE

www.pref.saitama.lg.jp

5

KUROSUKE (SOOT SPRITES) HOUSE

SAITAMA PREFECTURE

COORDINATES

35.79122, 139.40708

WEBSITE

www.totoro.or.jp

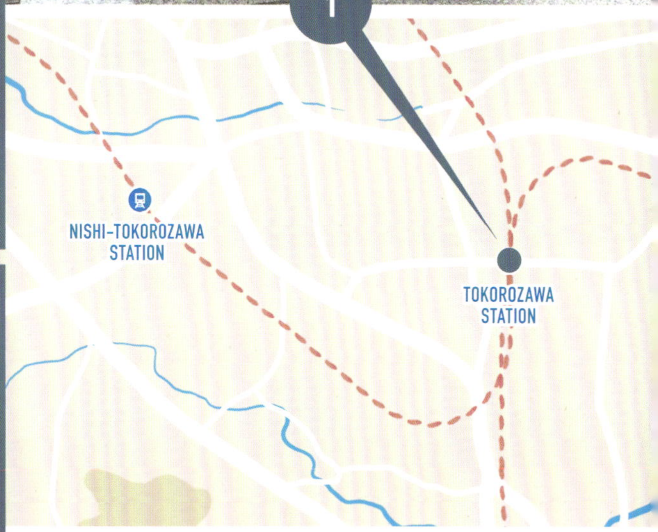

TOTORO STATUE

TOKOROZAWA STATION

The best way to get to **Totoro's forest** is to take a train at **JR Ikebukuro Station** heading toward **Seibukyujo-Mae Station**. You'll need to change trains at **Nishi-Tokorozawa** to continue to the end of the line. Just before **Nishi-Tokorozawa** is **Tokorozawa Station**, where you can hop off to visit the **Totoro statue**, either on your way there or on the way back.

TOTORO'S FOREST

This forest was created and is maintained by the **Totoro no Furusato Foundation (Totoro Fund)**. It is located in the hills of Saitama, about an hour by train from Tokyo. It measures nearly 7 miles from east to west and about 2.5 miles from north to south. The forested areas open to visitors are numbered (Totoro Forest No. 1, 2, and so on). The foundation's website offers details for a pleasant hour's walk from **Seibukyujo-Mae Station** to its headquarters at the **Kurosuke (Soot Sprites) House**.

HORIGUCHI TENMAN SHRINE

This small shrine is in the woods along the suggested route to the **Kurosuke (Soot Sprites) House**.

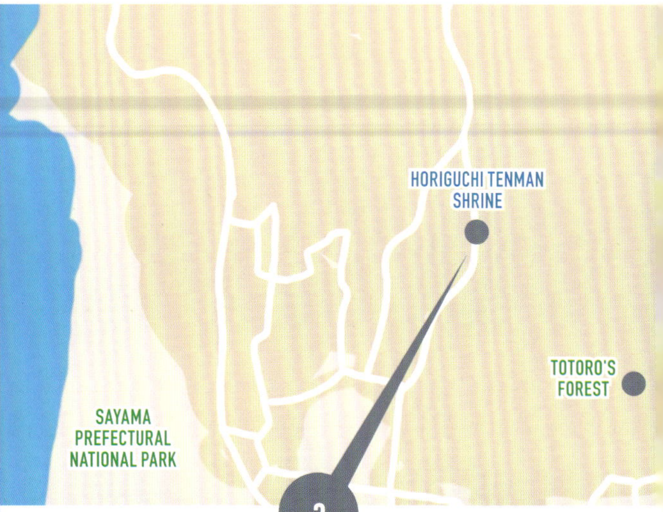

HORIGUCHI TENMAN SHRINE

TOTORO'S FOREST

SAYAMA PREFECTURAL NATIONAL PARK

3

SAYAMA LAKE

Near the end of your walk, before the **Kurosuke (Soot Sprites) House**, take a detour to the sprawling **Sayama Lake**, where you can enjoy the beautiful scenery of Saitama's valleys and use the public restrooms.

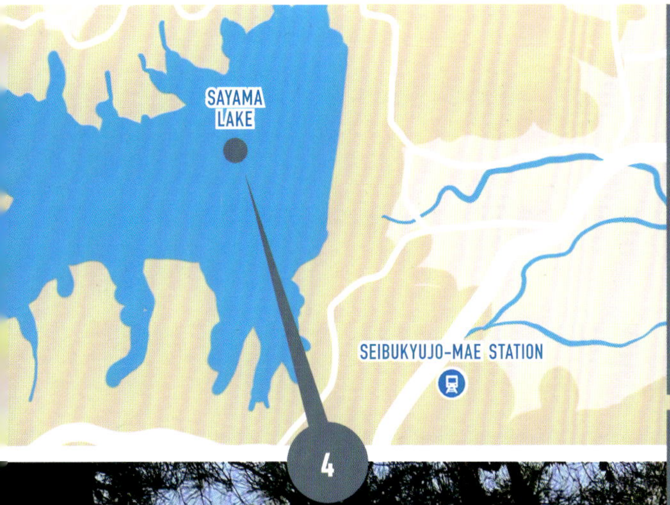

SAYAMA LAKE

SEIBUKYUJO-MAE STATION

4

KUROSUKE (SOOT SPRITES) HOUSE

The **Totoro no Furusato Foundation (Totoro Fund)** is based at this private home. A small shop sells Studio Ghibli souvenirs to raise funds. You'll also find a life-size statue of Totoro. There is a fee for admission, and reservations are required.

DEMON SLAYER: KIMETSU NO YAIBA

Tanjiro Kamado is a young boy turned demon slayer after his family is slaughtered by a demon. His sister Nezuko is the sole survivor of the massacre, but her fate is even more tragic: She has been transformed into a demon herself. Determined to find a cure for Nezuko and avenge his family, Tanjiro joins the Demon Slayer Corps, a secret organization whose mission is to eliminate demons. The story takes place in a fictional world inspired by the Taisho era (1912–1926), a period that marked the transition between Japan's Meiji and Showa eras.

The atmosphere of the time is still evident today in the natural settings and temples associated with each character. Japan's rural areas have changed far less than its urban ones. To really get into the spirit, visit the Meiji-Mura open-air museum, as well as the Asakusa district in Tokyo's Taito ward, where traces of Tokyo's past are still palpable. The street of shops leading to Senso-ji Temple feel like a step back in time.

DEMON SLAYER: KIMETSU NO YAIBA

HARUO SOTOZAKI (2019)

JAPAN

HAKODATE
AOMORI
HIROSAKI
AKITA
SAKATA
YAMAGATA
SENDAI
NIIGATA
NIIGATA
FUKUSHIMA
FUKUSHIMA
ISHIKAWA
KANAZAWA
GUNMA
TOCHIJI
IBARAKI
NAGANO
SAITAMA
GIFU
TOKYO
YAMANASHI
YOKOHAMA
CHIBA
TOTTORI
HYOGO
KYOTO
NAGOYA
AICHI
SHIZUOKA
SHIMANE
OKAYAMA
OSAKA
HIROSHIMA
MIE
YAMAGUCHI
KAGAWA
MATSUYAMA
TOKUSHIMA
WAKAYAMA
KOCHI
EHIME
KOCHI
FUKUOKA
SAGA
OITA
NAGASAKI
KUMAMOTO
MIYAZAKI
KAGOSHIMA
1
2
3
4
5
6
7
8

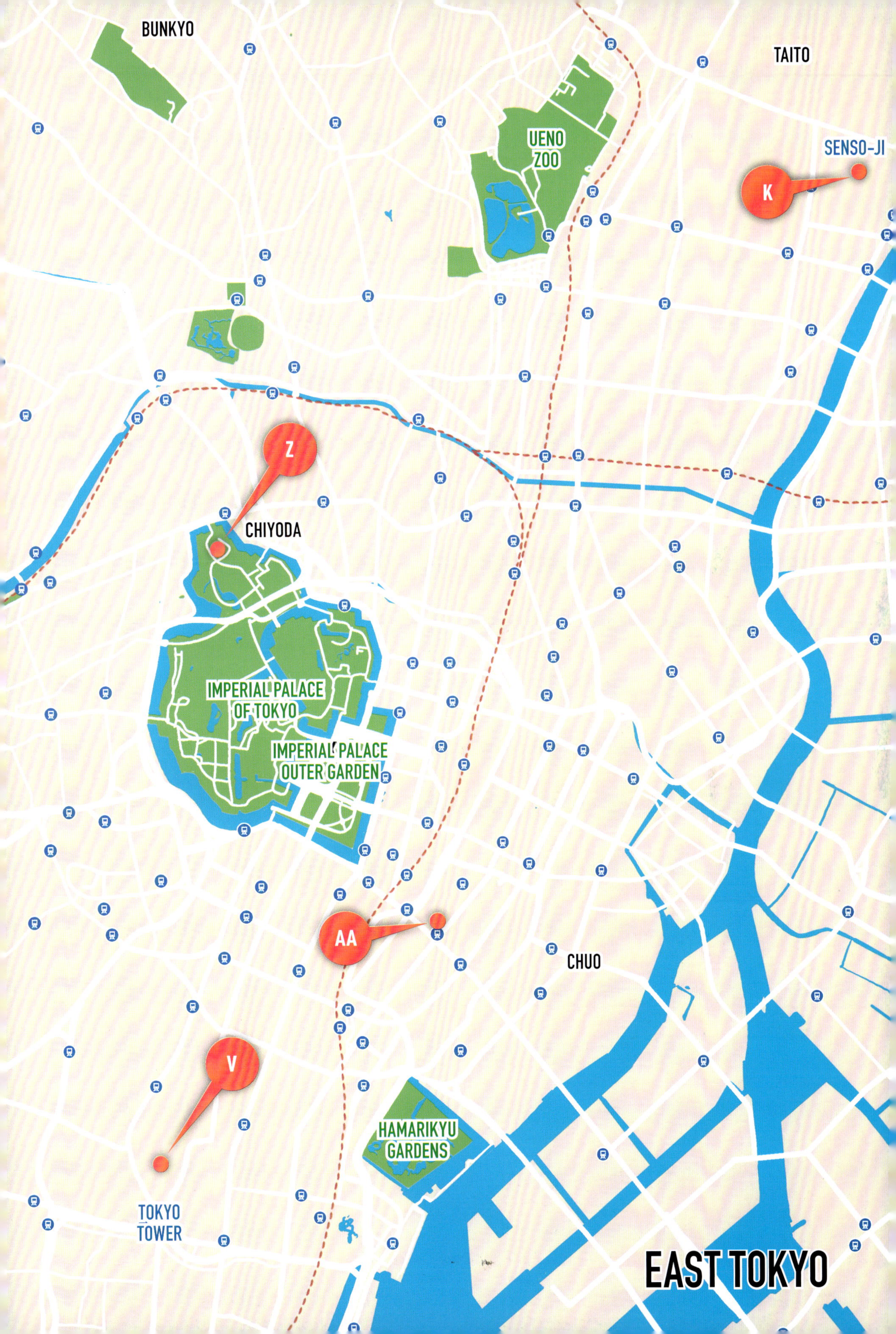

BUNKYO
TAITO
UENO ZOO
SENSO-JI
K
Z
CHIYODA
IMPERIAL PALACE OF TOKYO
IMPERIAL PALACE OUTER GARDEN
AA
CHUO
V
HAMARIKYU GARDENS
TOKYO TOWER
EAST TOKYO

1

MOUNT KUMOTORI
SAITAMA PREFECTURE

COORDINATES
35.85549, 138.94395

2

MOUNT ODAKE
NISHITAMA

COORDINATES
35.76514, 139.13046

3

MOUNT HINODE
NISHITAMA

COORDINATES
35.78116, 139.16747

4

MOUNT KAGENOBU
KANAGAWA PREFECTURE

COORDINATES
35.64594, 139.21581

5

AMENOIWATATE SHRINE
NARA PREFECTURE

COORDINATES
34.72671, 135.95943

6

KAMADO SHRINE
FUKUOKA PREFECTURE

COORDINATES
33.52883, 130.55253

WEBSITE
www.pref.saitama.lg.jp

7

ASHIKAGA FLOWER PARK
TOCHIGI PREFECTURE

COORDINATES
36.31415, 139.52002

WEBSITE
www.ashikaga.co.jp

K

SENSO-JI TEMPLE

TAITO

COORDINATES

35.71476, 139.79665

WEBSITE

www.senso-ji.jp

8

MEIJI-MURA MUSEUM

AICHI PREFECTURE

COORDINATES

35.34044, 136.98852

WEBSITE

www.meijimura.com

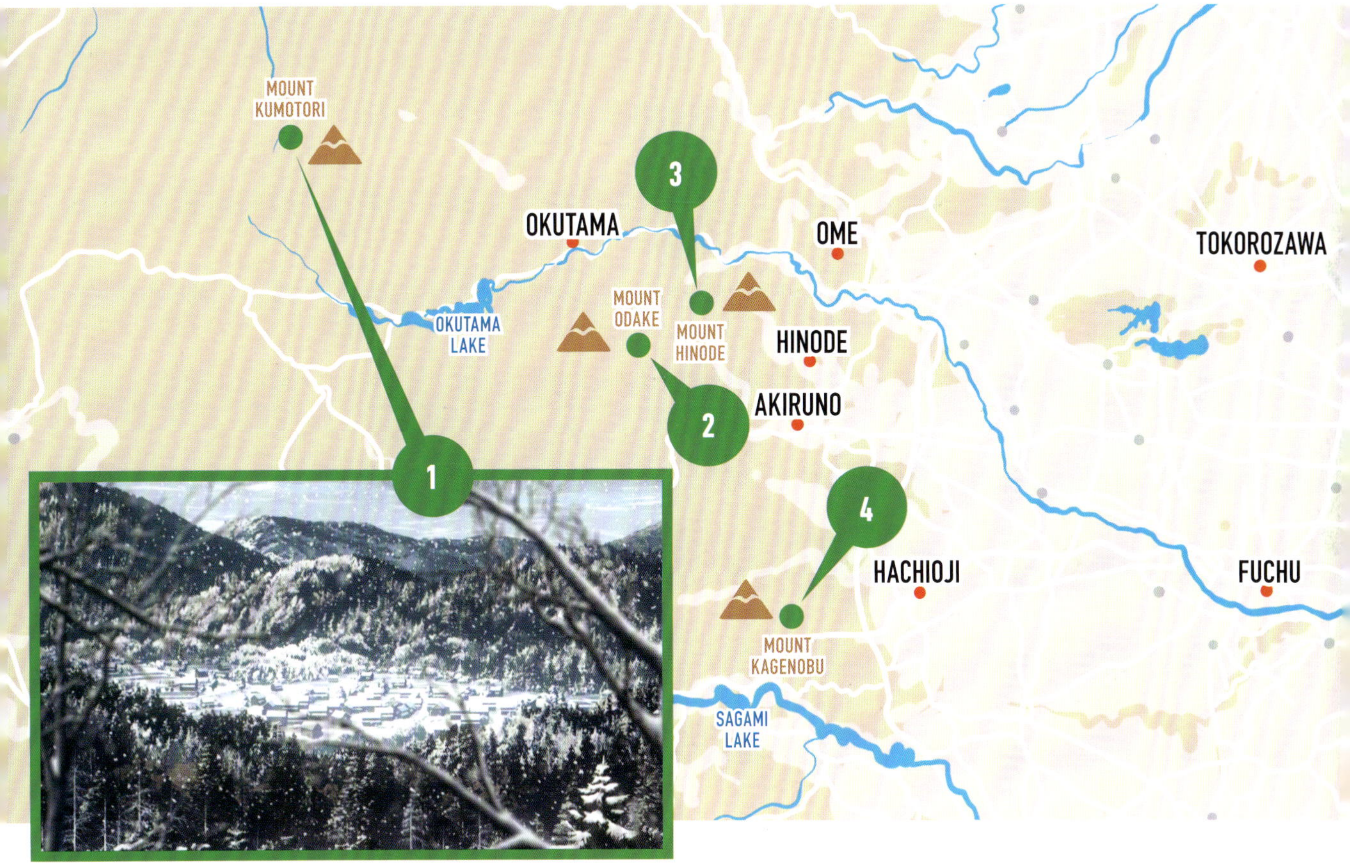

MOUNT KUMOTORI
3
OKUTAMA
OME
TOKOROZAWA
OKUTAMA LAKE
MOUNT ODAKE
MOUNT HINODE
HINODE
AKIRUNO
2
1
4
HACHIOJI
FUCHU
MOUNT KAGENOBU
SAGAMI LAKE

MOUNT KUMOTORI, MOUNT ODAKE, MOUNT HINODE & MOUNT KAGENOBU

These four mountains are the birthplaces of **Tanjiro** and **Nezuko**, **Inosuke Hashibira** (Tanjiro's traveling companion, who was raised by boars), **Gyomei Himejima** (the Stone Hashira), and **Muichiro Tokito** (the Mist Hashira), respectively.

Along the path to **Mount Kagenobu**, where Muichiro Tokito was born, are stalls selling novelties and souvenirs.

AMENOIWATATE & KAMADO SHRINES

EPISODE 3

Near **Amenoiwatate Shrine** (5) is a giant boulder that has been split in half. Legend has it that the stone was cleaved with a sword by Yagyu Munetoshi while fighting a *tengu*. **Kamado Shrine** (6), which shares Tanjiro's family name, has become a pilgrimage site for fans because it is located near the hometown of the original manga artist for the series.

ASHIKAGA FLOWER PARK

EPISODE 4

This park is famous for its majestic wisteria, a flower known for repelling demons. Wisterias appear in the manga when Tanjiro takes the final exam to become a member of the Demon Slayer Corps.

7

TAITO

UENO ZOO

UENO STATION

ASAKUSA STATION

SENSO-JI TEMPLE

SUMIDA RIVER

K

SENSO-JI TEMPLE

EPISODE 7

This is where Tanjiro initially encounters Muzan Kibutsuji, the first demon in existence and the source of all evil in the world. The two cross paths in the commercial streets surrounding Senso-ji Temple in Asakusa, clearly set in the Taisho era. However, even today, many places in the neighborhood feel as if they are frozen in time.

MEIJI-MURA MUSEUM

EPISODE 23 - *DEMON SLAYER: KIMETSU NO YAIBA—THE MOVIE: MUGEN TRAIN*

This open-air museum preserves and restores historical buildings from the Meiji era (1868–1912). Tanjiro lives in the Taisho era (1912–1926), so the museum gives visitors a feel for his world. The **Butterfly Mansion**, where Tanjiro stays in Episode 23, closely resembles the **Japan Red Cross Society Central Hospital**. The park is also home to several locomotives reminiscent of the Mugen Train in the 2020 film ***Demon Slayer: Kimetsu no Yaiba—The Movie: Mugen Train***.

8

IRUKA LAKE

MEIJI-MURA MUSEUM

8

CREAMY MAMI, THE MAGICAL ANGEL

Yuu Morisawa is a ten-year-old girl living in Kurimigaoka. One day, she spots a mysterious boat in the sky that is caught in a dream storm. As she approaches, a force pulls her aboard, inadvertently helping an alien named Pino Pino find his way back aboard the *Feather Star*. In return, Pino Pino gives Yuu a magic wand that she can use for one year. Two magical cats, Posi and Nega, are tasked with accompanying her. With their help, Yuu quickly learns to use the wand's powers, which allow her to transform into a sixteen-year-old girl. Thanks to her new identity, she becomes a famous singer and quickly rises to stardom as the popular idol Creamy Mami. Her crush, Toshio, becomes a huge Creamy fan but doesn't realize that Yuu and Creamy are the same person. Thus begins Yuu's double life, split between school during the day and the spotlight when her homework is done.

Creamy's hectic life supposedly takes place in Tokyo, but there are few references to the real city. Some landmarks, such as **Korakuen Stadium** (which no longer exists) and **Nippon Budokan**, make appearances, but her adventures take her all over Japan.

CREAMY MAMI, THE MAGICAL ANGEL

OSAMU KOBAYASHI (1983)

52 EPISODES

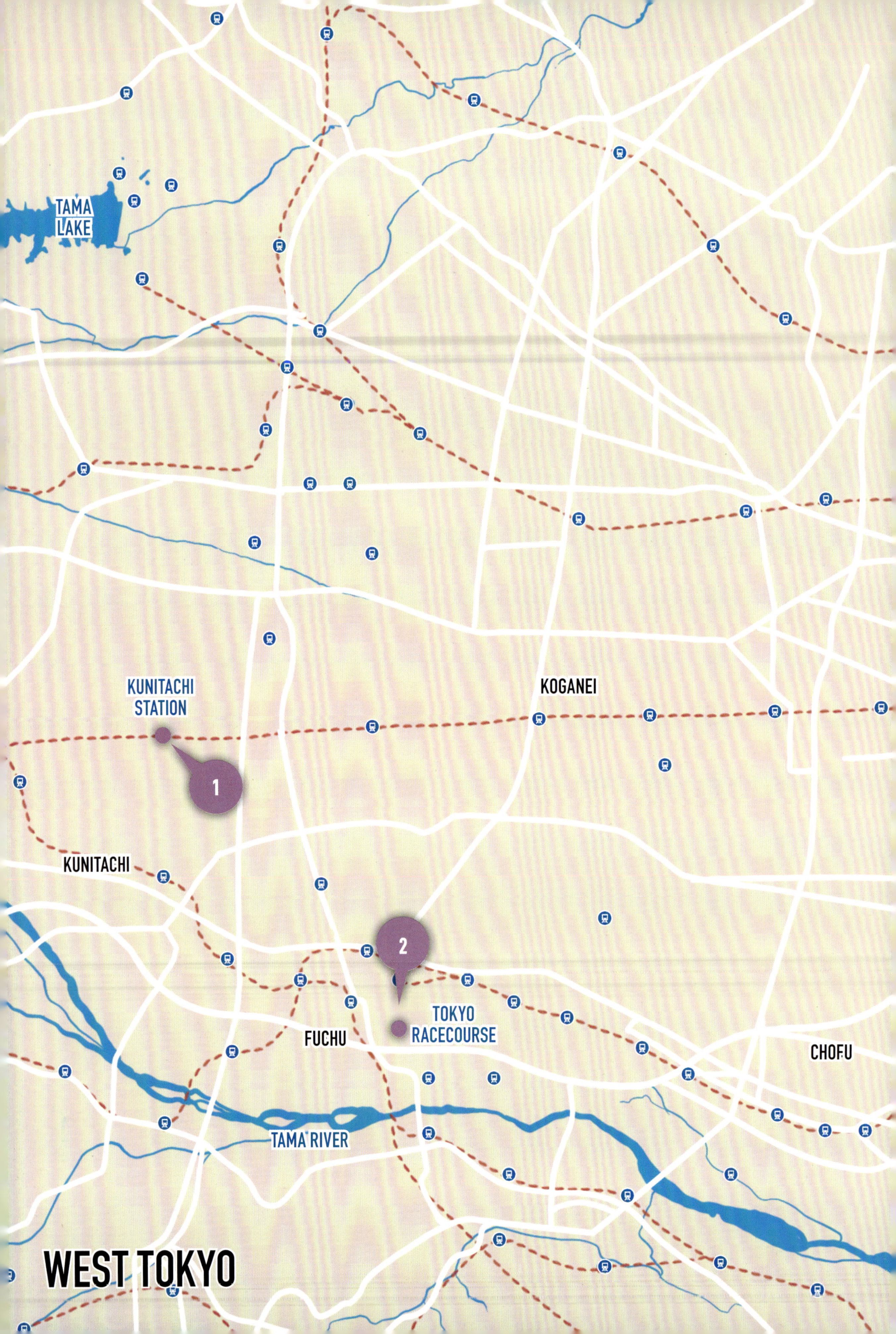
TAMA LAKE
KUNITACHI STATION
1
KOGANEI
KUNITACHI
2
TOKYO RACECOURSE
FUCHU
CHOFU
TAMA RIVER
WEST TOKYO

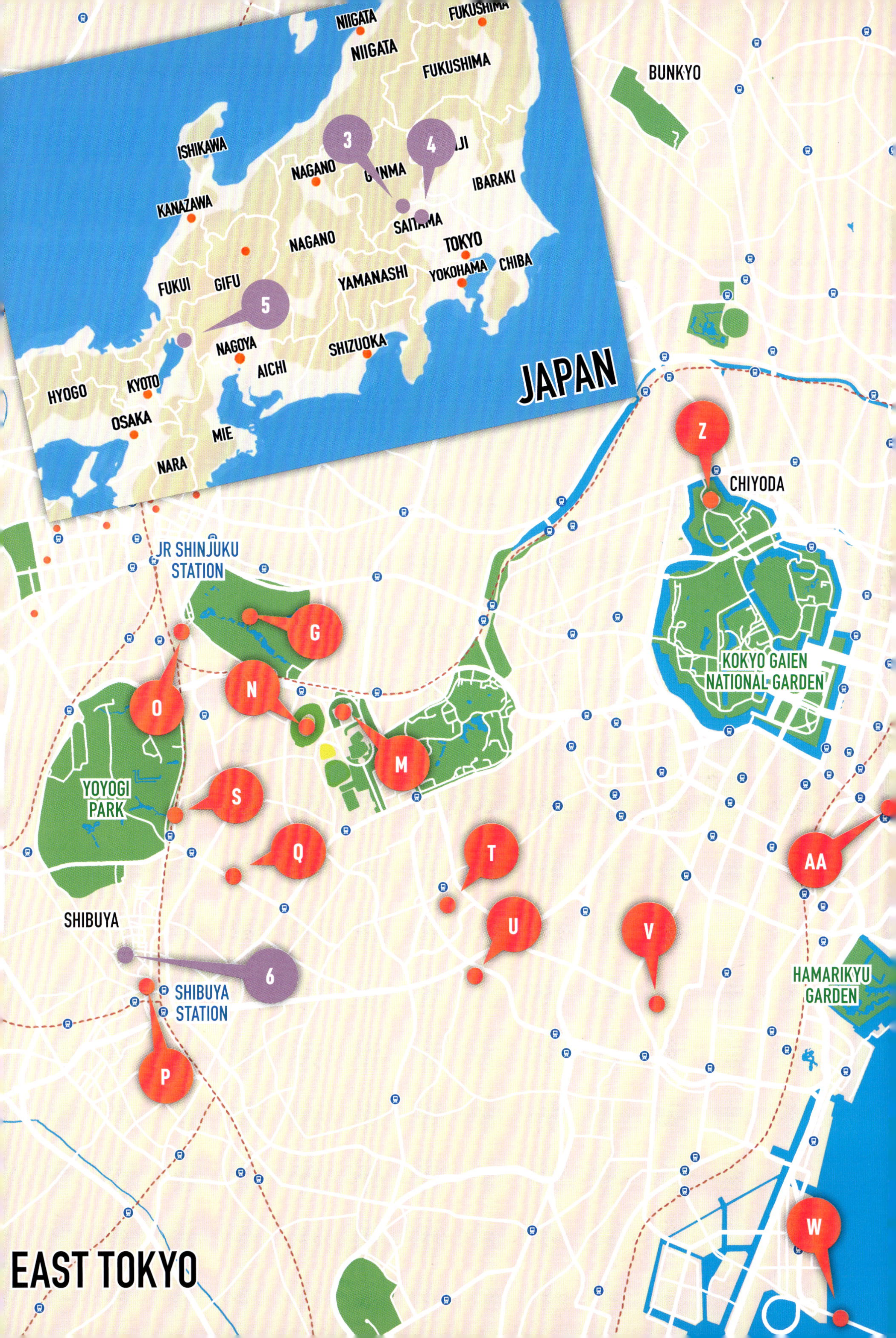

JAPAN
NIIGATA
FUKUSHIMA
ISHIKAWA
NAGANO
GUNMA
IBARAKI
KANAZAWA
SAITAMA
TOKYO
FUKUI
GIFU
YAMANASHI
YOKOHAMA
CHIBA
NAGOYA
AICHI
SHIZUOKA
HYOGO
KYOTO
OSAKA
MIE
NARA
BUNKYO
CHIYODA
JR SHINJUKU STATION
KOKYO GAIEN NATIONAL GARDEN
YOYOGI PARK
SHIBUYA
SHIBUYA STATION
HAMARIKYU GARDEN
EAST TOKYO

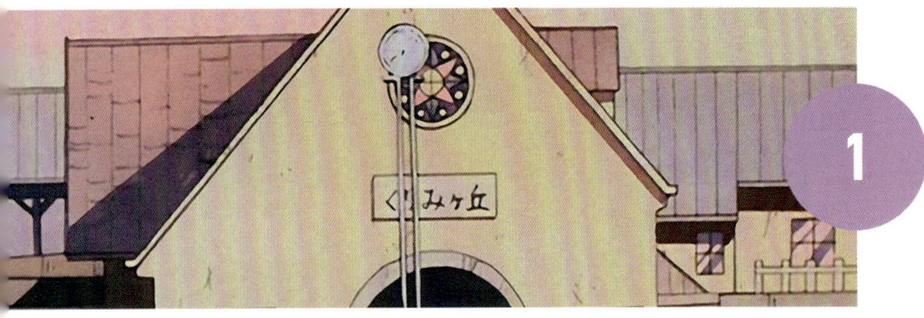

1

KUNITACHI STATION

KUNITACHI, TOKYO

COORDINATES

35.69929, 139.44602

2

TOKYO RACECOURSE

FUCHU, TOKYO

COORDINATES

35.66522, 139.48482

WEBSITE

www.jra.go.jp

3

NIPPARA LIMESTONE CAVES

NIPPARA, NISHITAMA DISTRICT

COORDINATES

35.85245, 139.04075

WEBSITE

www.nippara.com

4

ISHIBUNE BRIDGE

TOKURA, AKIRUNO, TOKYO

COORDINATES

35.7266, 139.1897

WEBSITE

www.pref.saitama.lg.jp

5

TOGENDAI STATION

HAKONE, KANAGAWA

COORDINATES

35.23787, 138.99457

WEBSITE

www.hakoneropeway.co.jp

6

PARCO

SHIBUYA

COORDINATES

35.66204, 139.69877

WEBSITE

travel.gaijinpot.com/shibuya-parco/

Z

NIPPON BUDOKAN

CHIYODA

COORDINATES

35.69333, 139.7497

WEBSITE

www.nipponbudokan.or.jp

KUNITACHI STATION & TOKYO RACECOURSE

EPISODE 1

Kurimigaoka is a small fictional town outside Tokyo where Yuu lives with her family. The town is inspired by the real-life town of Kunitachi. Its old train station, recognizable in the anime, was demolished in 2006 and rebuilt in the same style in 2020. Tokyo Racecourse, where Yuu meets Pino Pino, is located in the neighboring city of Fuchu and has also been renovated.

NIPPARA LIMESTONE CAVES

EPISODE 6

Called the Moppara Caves in the anime, these are the largest caves in the Kanto region. They feature spectacular stalactites and stalagmites that have taken centuries to form, as well as a half-mile path with a fabulous light show playing across the limestone. Relaxing music was recently added to the experience.

ISHIBUNE BRIDGE

EPISODE 6

The film crew for Creamy's promotional video visits the **Akigawa Valley** (called the Natsukawa Valley in the series). The 320-foot-long Ishibune Bridge spans the **Aki River** in **Chichibu-Tama-Kai** National Park. The view of Akigawa Valley is truly breathtaking.

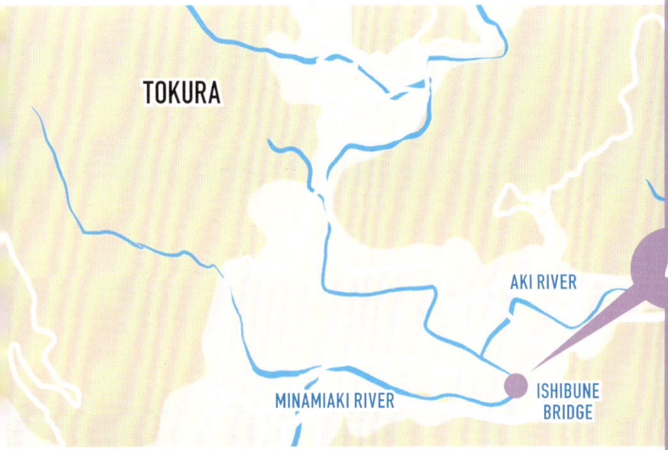

TOKURA

AKI RIVER

4

MINAMIAKI RIVER

ISHIBUNE BRIDGE

4

NII-JIMA TO TOKYO

EPISODE 19

Creamy is scheduled to perform at Korakuen Stadium in Tokyo but finds herself in Nii-jima **(A)**. The entire episode is a race against time to reach the concert venue by evening. Creamy and her manager, Hayato Kidokoro, first fly to Osaka on a commercial flight **(A)** and then take a bullet train **(B)** toward Tokyo, but it breaks down in Shizuoka **(C)**. They pick up a minibus borrowed from a group of Creamy fans and head for Atami **(D)**. They arrive at Lake Ashi **(E)** in Hakone **(F)** in Kanagawa Prefecture, where Creamy parts ways with Hayato and boards a sightseeing boat that crosses Lake Ashinoko (**www.hakonenavi.jp**).

Creamy disembarks at Togendai Station **(5)** by the **Hakone Ropeway** and, as Yuu, takes the cable car to Sounzan Station **(35.24666, 139.03554)**. From there, she takes a train through **Gora** in Hakone Yumoto **(G)** to Yokohama **(H)** and then finally to **Shinjuku**, arriving at Korakuen Stadium **(I)** just in time for the concert.

In 2020, the **NERV** headquarters from the anime *Neon Genesis Evangelion* was recreated in parts of Togendai Station. There's also a replica of the **EVA-01** unit.

TOGENDAI STATION

ASHINOKO LAKE

HAKONE

KORAKUEN STADIUM

EPISODE 19

The stadium was officially closed on November 8, 1987, and was demolished shortly afterward to make way for a skyscraper, the **Tokyo Dome Hotel**. The remaining area was transformed into a plaza with entrances to the **Tokyo Dome**.

PARCO

EPISODE 25

Department stores such as **Parco** in **Shibuya** frequently open pop-up stores and organize themed events featuring pop artists. In the winter of 2023, one was dedicated entirely to Hayao Miyazaki's ***Howl's Moving Castle***.

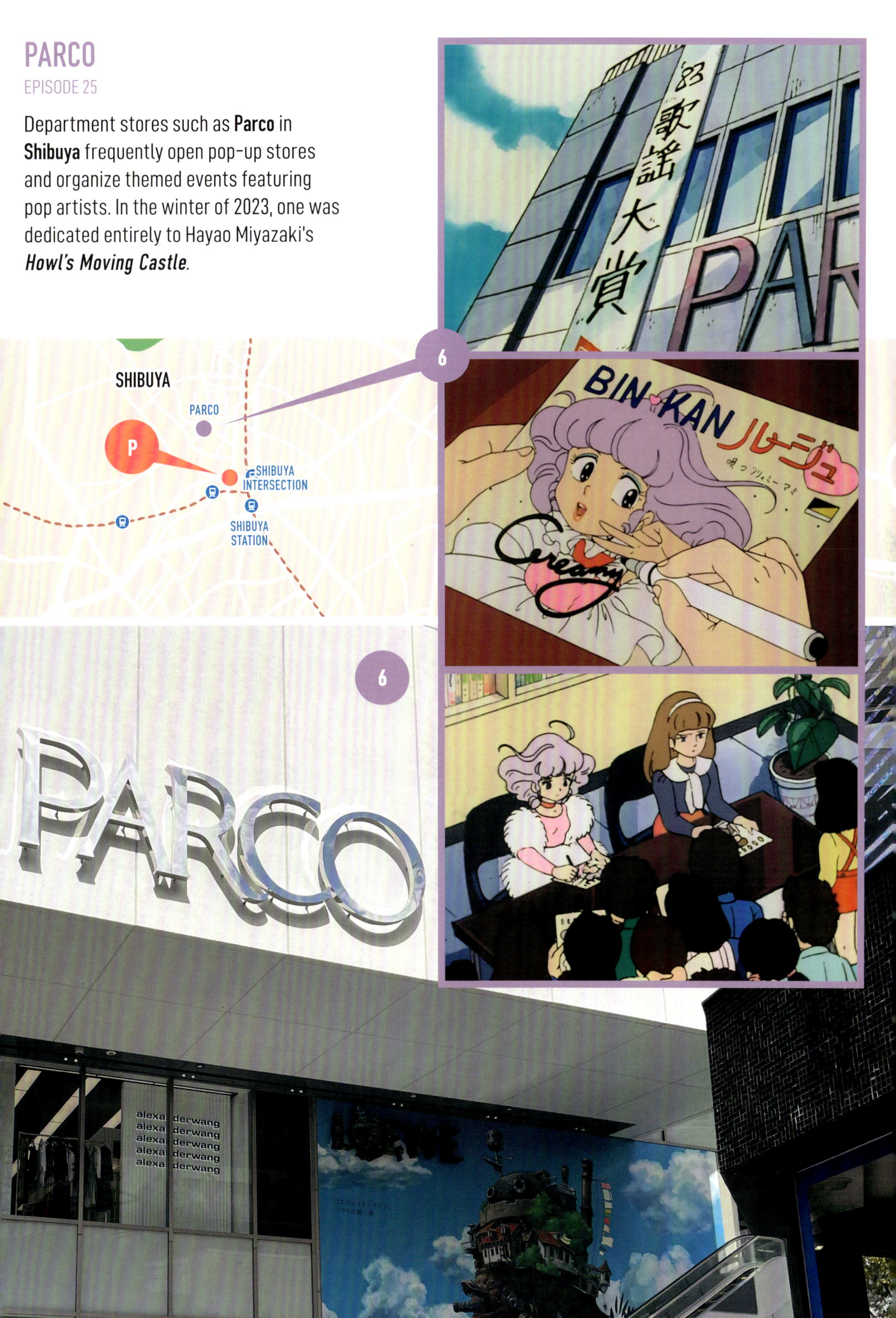

NIPPON BUDOKAN

EPISODES 25 & 26

Toshio discovers Creamy's secret during the **NPB Pops Festival** at **Nippon Budokan**, which was originally a sports arena but is also used for concerts and other large-scale events.

NERIMA

The success of **Toei Animation** (formerly Toei Doga) began in 1958 with ***The White Snake Enchantress***, the studio's first feature-length, color, animated film. Toei's offices were located in the Oizumigakuencho district, so the movie put Nerima ward on the map. A few years later, in 1963, local resident Osamu Tezuka founded **Mushi Production** (now defunct, although the building still stands in the Fujimidai district) and produced ***Astro Boy***, whose massive success set the standard for Japanese animation for years to come.

Even today, Nerima remains home to numerous animation studios. In addition to **Toei Animation** (www.toei-anim.co.jp), past and current studios include **Studio Gallop** (www.anime-gallop.co.jp), **Studio Comet** (http://st-comet.com), **Anime International Company** (www.anime-int.com), **Studio Nue** (creators of ***Macross***), and **Office Academy** (creators of ***Yamato***, set in Toyotama Kita). Popular anime such as ***One Piece***, ***Dragon Ball***, and ***Pretty Cure*** were all made there.

Nerima has been a hub for many creators. **Yoshiyuki Tomino** joined **Mushi Production** after graduating from Nihon University College of Art in Nerima, and young talents **Yoshikazu Yasuhiko**, **Hayao Miyazaki**, and **Isao Takahata** also worked at Tezuka Productions.

The area has inspired many a well-known manga author, including **Leiji Matsumoto** and **Rumiko Takahashi**, who drew inspiration from local streets for their works.

NERIMA
THE BIRTHPLACE OF ANIME

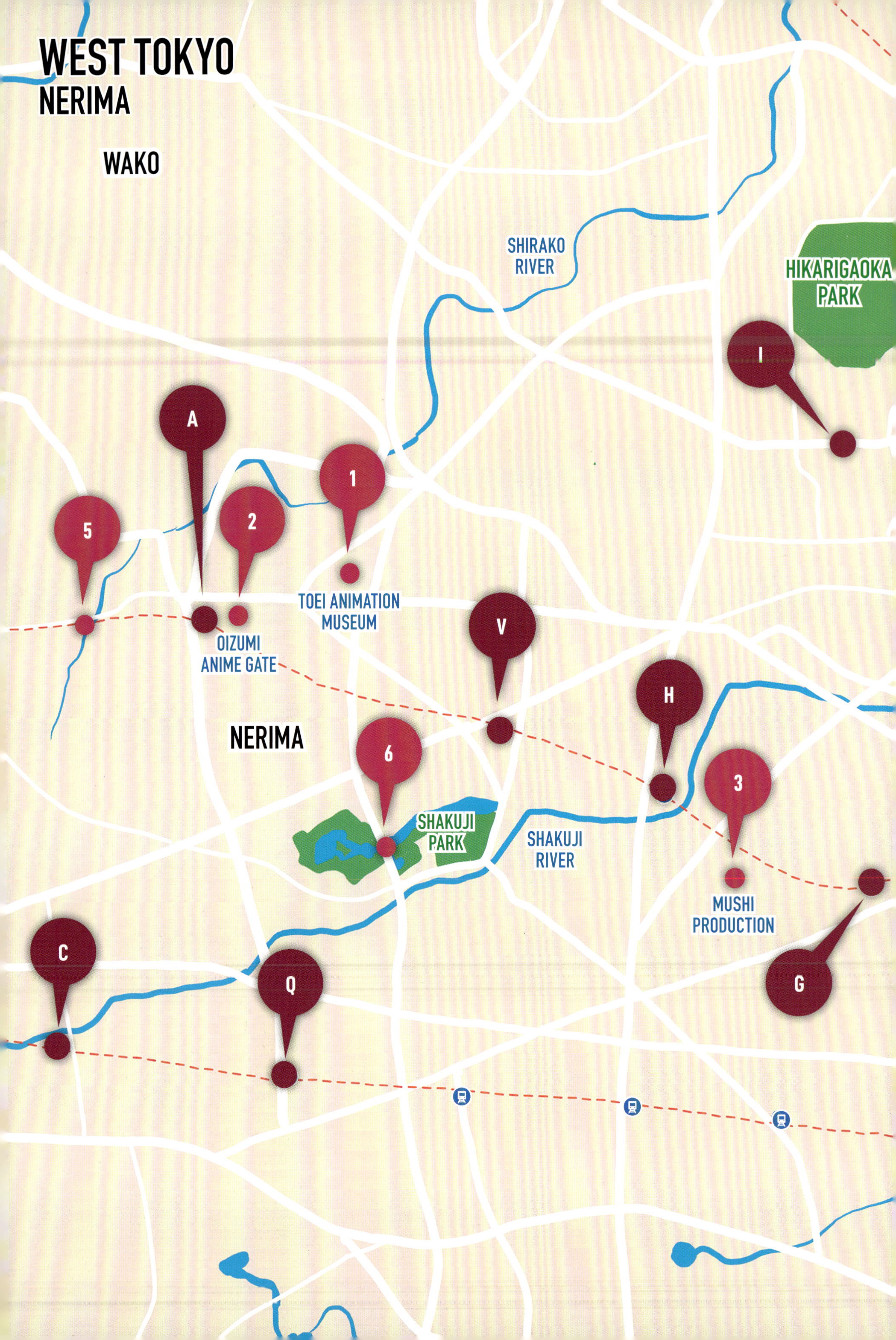

WEST TOKYO
NERIMA
WAKO
SHIRAKO RIVER
HIKARIGAOKA PARK
I
A
1
2
5
TOEI ANIMATION MUSEUM
OIZUMI ANIME GATE
V
H
NERIMA
6
3
SHAKUJI PARK
SHAKUJI RIVER
MUSHI PRODUCTION
C
Q
G

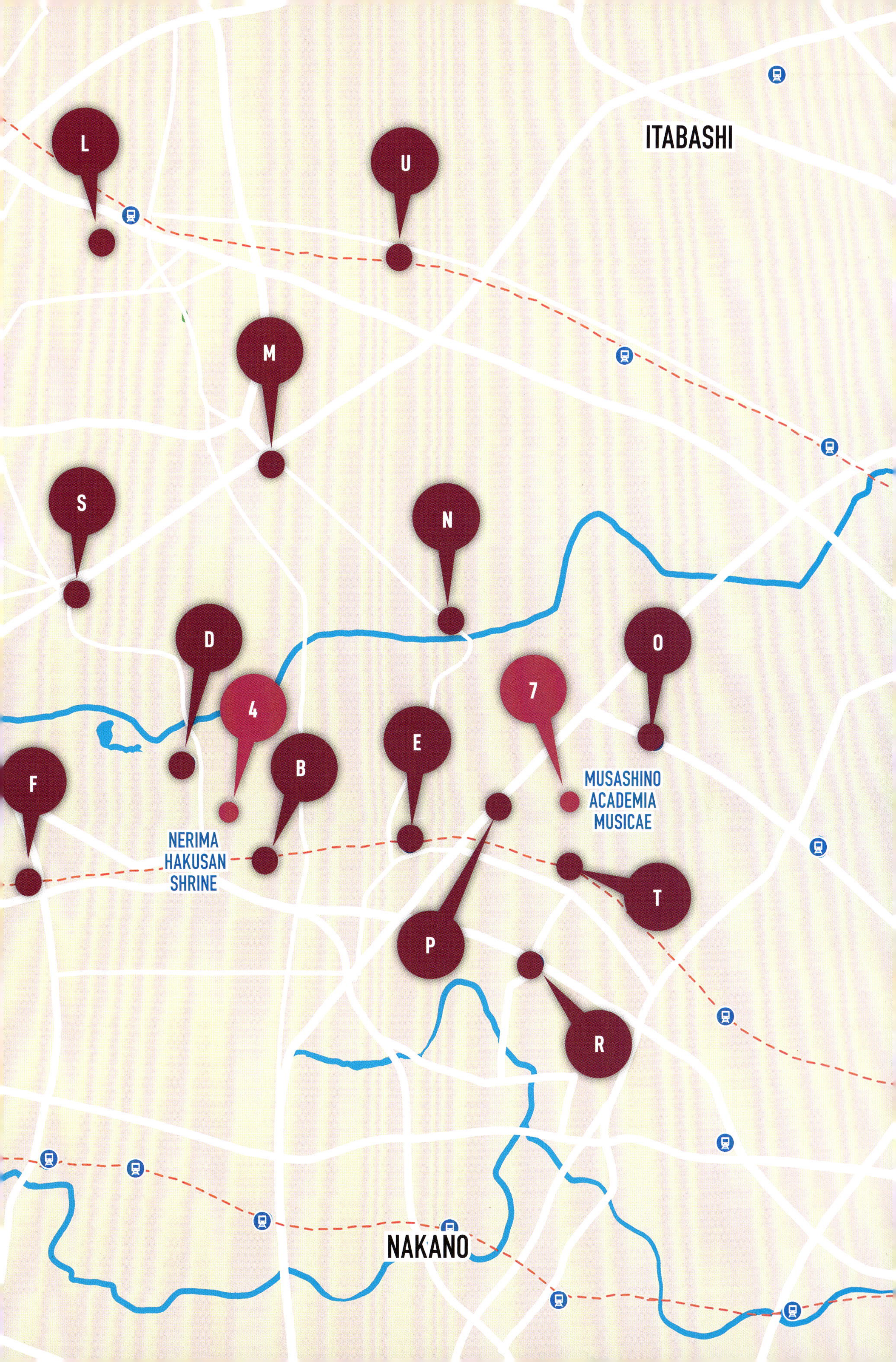
ITABASHI
L
U
M
S
N
D
O
4
7
E
B
F
MUSASHINO
ACADEMIA
MUSICAE
NERIMA
HAKUSAN
SHRINE
T
P
R
NAKANO

1 TOEI ANIMATION MUSEUM

NERIMA, TOKYO

COORDINATES
35.75238, 139.59451

WEBSITE
museum.toei-anim.co.jp

2 OIZUMI ANIME GATE

NERIMA, TOKYO

COORDINATES
35.74964, 139.58683

WEBSITE
animation-nerima.jp

3 MUSHI PRODUCTION CO. LTD.

NERIMA, TOKYO

COORDINATES
35.73572, 139.62149

4 NERIMA HAKUSAN SHRINE

NERIMA, TOKYO

COORDINATES
35.74067, 139.65031

WEBSITE
www.nerimahakusan.or.jp

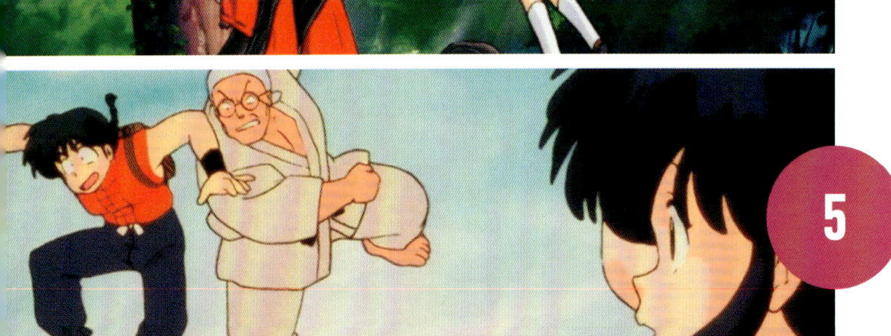

5 SHIRAKO RIVER

NERIMA, TOKYO

COORDINATES
35.74947, 139.57903

6 SHAKUJII PARK

NERIMA, TOKYO

COORDINATES
35.73795, 139.59899

WEBSITE
www.tokyo-park.or.jp

7 MUSASHINO ACADEMIA MUSICAE

NERIMA, TOKYO

COORDINATES
35.74124, 139.6721

WEBSITE
www.musashino-music.ac.jp

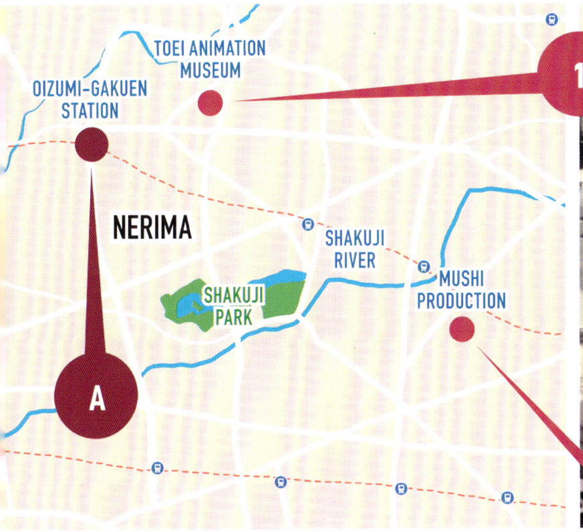

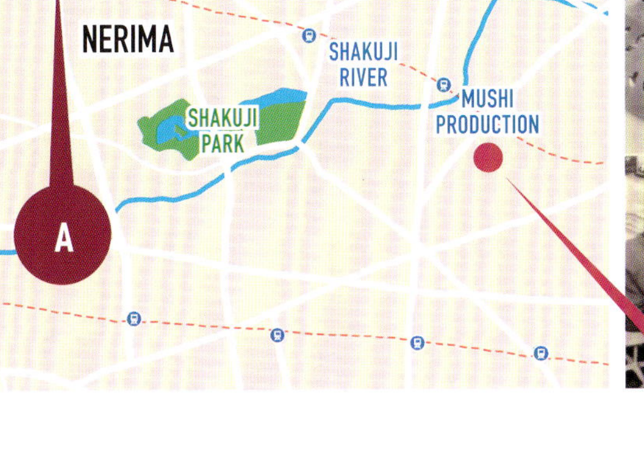

TOEI ANIMATION MUSEUM & MUSHI PRODUCTION

The **Toei Animation Museum**, which opened in 2018, offers only a glimpse into **Toei Animation's** influence. Unfortunately, the production studios behind the museum are not open to the public. As for **Mushi Production**, the only remaining structure is an old, abandoned building, but it's still worth a stroll around the area, for nostalgia's sake.

ANIME STATIONS

In honor of its anime history, twenty of Nerima ward's metro and train stations are dedicated to iconic characters created locally. Below is a list of the stations and the anime they honor. The first station features the largest display; the others display only commemorative plaques.

A - OIZUMI-GAKUEN - *GALAXY EXPRESS 999 / GINGA TETSUDO 999* (1978)

B - NERIMA - *THE WHITE SNAKE ENCHANTRESS / HAKUJADEN* (1958)

C - MUSASHI-SEKI - *IKKYU-SAN* (1975)

D - TOSHIMAEN - *YES! PRECURE 5 GOGO!* (2007)

E - SAKURADAI - *CYBORG 009* (1966)

F - NAKAMURABASHI - *GEGEGE NO KITARO* (1968)

G - FUJIMIDAI - *ASTRO BOY / TETSUWAN ATOM* (1963)

H - NERIMA-TAKANODAI - *ASHITA NO JOE / ASHITA NO JO* (1970)

I - HIKARIGAOKA - *DIGIMON ADVENTURE* (1999)

J - AKATSUKA (METRO) – *AKKO-CHAN'S GOT A SECRET! / HIMITSU NO AKKO-CHAN* (1969)

K - HEIWADAI - *KIMBA THE WHITE LION / JANGURU TAITEI* (1965)

L - HIKAWADAI - *SARUTOBI ECCHAN* (1971)

M - KOTAKE-MUKAIHARA - *BRAVE STORY* (2006)

N - SHIN-SAKURADAI - *MAGICAL DOREMI / OJAMAJO DOREMI* (1999)

O - KAMI-SHAKUJII – *SUPER DIMENSION FORTRESS MACROSS / CHOJIKU YOSAI MAKUROSU* (1982)

P - SHIN-EGOTA - *KOMANEKO* (2003)

Q - NERIMA-KASUGACHO - *NERIMA DAIKON BROTHERS / OROSHITATE MYUJIKARU NERIMA DAIKON BURAZAZU* (2006)

R - EKODA - *NODAME CANTABILE / NODAME KANTABIRE* (2007)

S - TOBU-NERIMA - *SALLY THE WITCH / MAHOTSUKAI SARI* (1966)

T - SHAKUJII-KOEN - *THE GUTSY FROG / DOKONJO GAERU* (1972)

H
I

J
K

L

M

N

O

P

5'0"
Q

R

S

T

OIZUMI ANIME GATE

Upon exiting the station, you can't miss the green space studded with life-size statues immortalizing some of the most iconic characters in Japanese animation. All the characters shown were born in Nerima because either their creators or their production companies were based there. The statues include **Astro Boy** from the series of the same name, Tetsuro and Maetel from ***Galaxy Express 999***, Joe Yabuki from ***Ashita No Joe***, and Lum from ***Urusei Yatsura***. The site also features informational plaques that pay tribute to the many famous series produced in Nerima. An annual festival, the **Anime Project in Oizumi**, is a gathering point for anime fans to enjoy a day of exhibitions, interviews, and workshops held around the station.

2

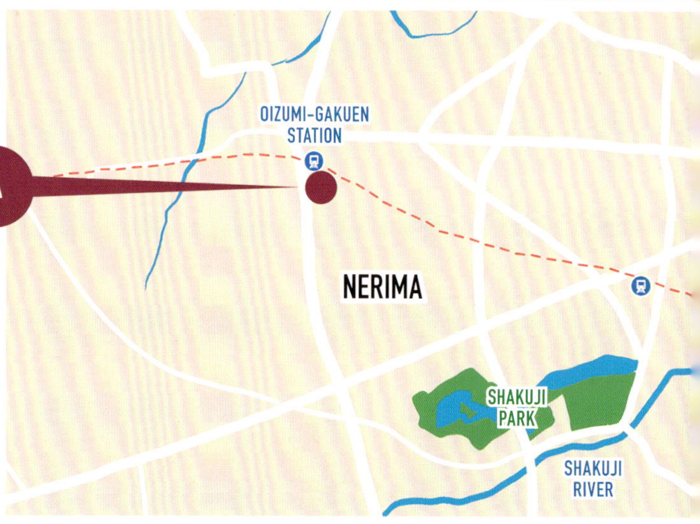

OIZUMI-GAKUEN STATION

GALAXY EXPRESS 999

Leiji Matsumoto moved to Nerima at the age of 25 and lived there until his death in 2023. In 2008, he became an "honored citizen" of Nerima; in 2015, he was added to the **Oizumi Anime Gate** project. The city memorialized him by erecting a statue of the **Conductor** at **Oizumi-Gakuen** station, along with several themed manhole covers, seven street lamps with a model of the famous train, and a mural painted on a railway fence across from the station.

INUYASHA
NERIMA HAKUSAN SHRINE
EPISODE 1

This small shrine a few minutes' walk from **Nerima Station** was the inspiration for Rumiko Takahashi's sacred tree in *Inuyasha*. The tree is a Japanese zelkova that is nearly nine hundred years old, standing forty-five feet tall and measuring more than twenty-three feet in circumference.

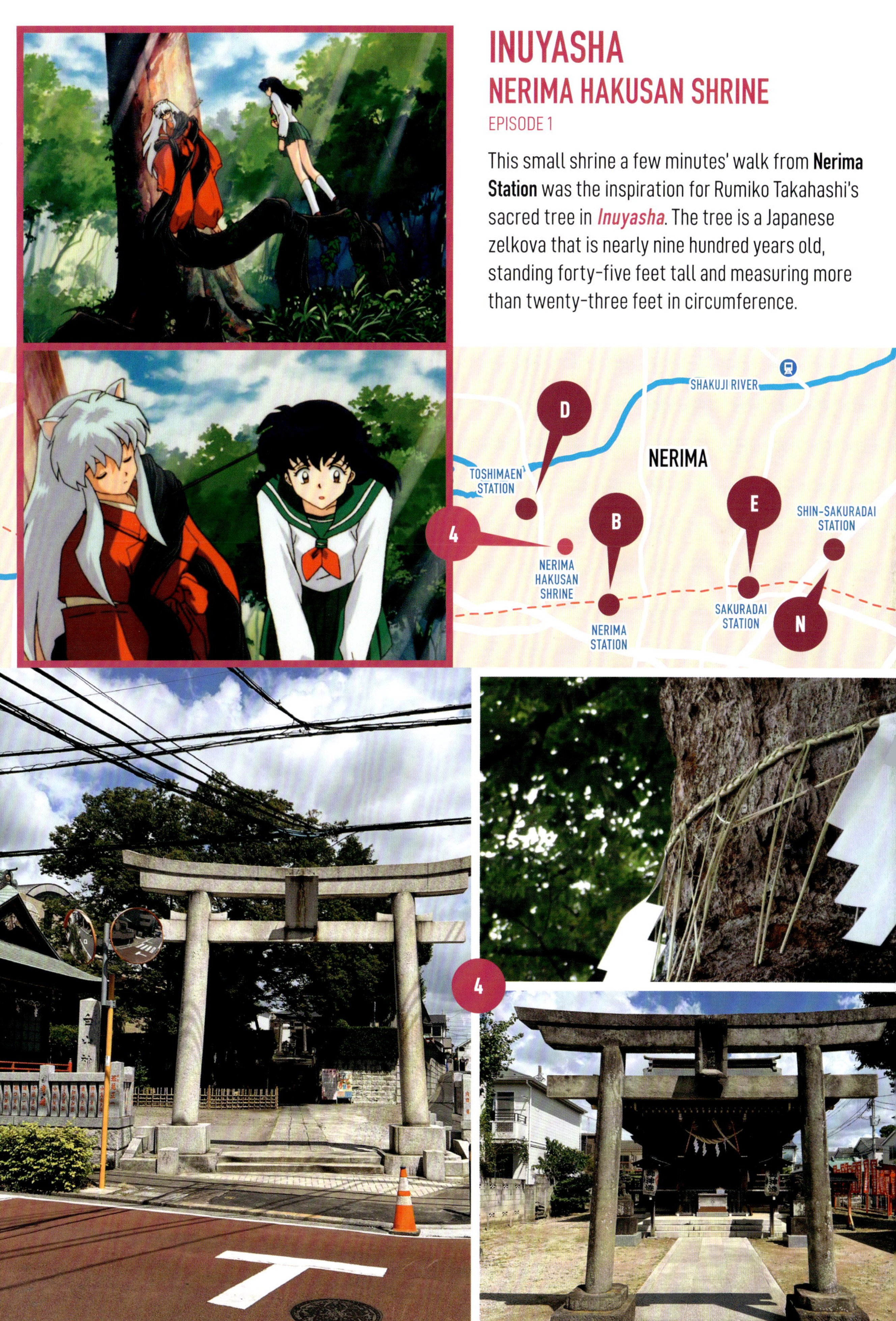

RANMA 1/2

SHIRAKO RIVER & SHAKUJII PARK

Shirako River and **Shakujii Park** appear frequently in the series ***Ranma ½***. Both are located near **Oizumi-Gakuen Station**. If you're in the vicinity of Nerima, these are two great spots for getting into the anime spirit.

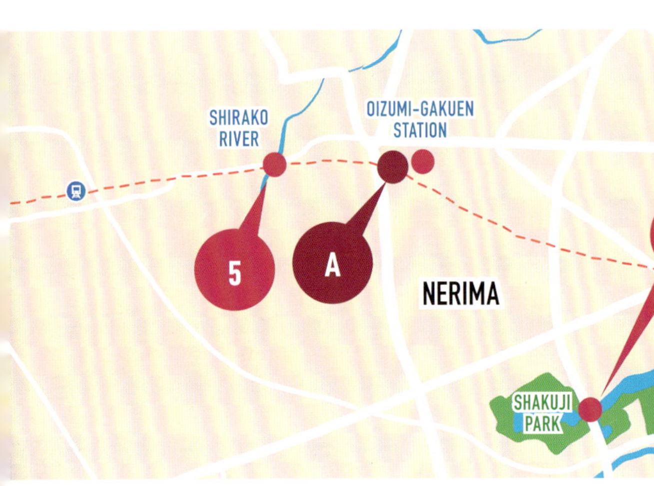

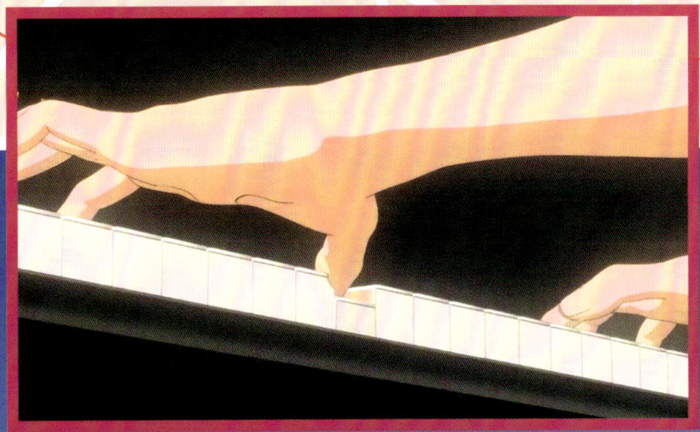

NODAME CANTABILE

MUSASHINO ACADEMIA MUSICAE

Near **Ekoda Station (R)**, which was named for *Nodame Cantabile*, is the **Musashino Academia Musicae**, the inspiration for the Momogaoka music school that the protagonists attend. The real-life school was renovated in 2015.

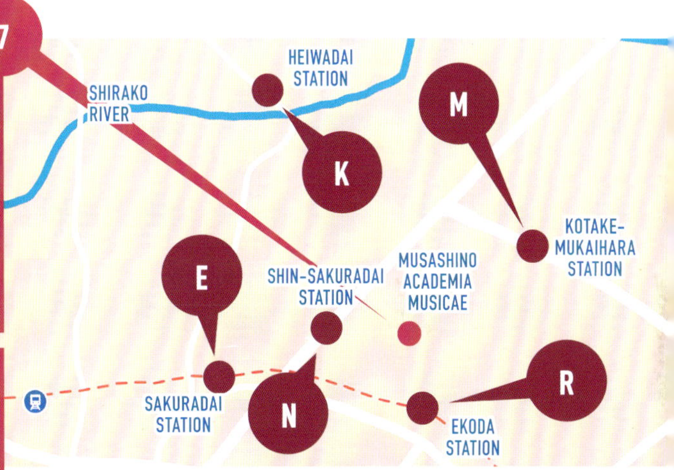

7
HEIWADAI STATION
SHIRAKO RIVER
M
K
KOTAKE-MUKAIHARA STATION
E
SHIN-SAKURADAI STATION
MUSASHINO ACADEMIA MUSICAE
R
SAKURADAI STATION
N
EKODA STATION

A

TOKYO METROPOLITAN GOVERNMENT BUILDING

One tower is divided into two sections, each with a panoramic observation deck offering incredible views of the city. Access to the platforms is free.

B

SOMPO BUILDING

With forty-three stories and standing six hundred fifty feet tall, this is one of the tallest buildings in Tokyo. Its geometric shape resembles a prism, giving it a modern, minimalist aesthetic.

C

SUMITOMO BUILDING

Completed in 1974, this fifty-two-story building (with an additional four underground levels) is home to offices, shops, and three restaurants.

D

TOKYO MODE GAKUEN (COCOON TOWER)

Designed by architect Kenzo Tange shortly before his death and completed by his firm, the tower stands 666 feet tall and is fifty stories high. It is home to a fashion school, a design school, and a medical school.

E

STUDIO ALTA (SHINJUKU DAIBIRU)

A nine-story building is known for a giant LED screen that plays video clips and commercials. The tower houses shops and numerous cafés and restaurants that offer something for everyone, from traditional Japanese dishes to cuisines from around the world. In 2000, the building changed owners and names, but fans still refer to it as Studio Alta.

F

SHINJUKU PARK TOWER

This skyscraper consists of three towers of varying heights. It became famous in 2003 as the setting for *Lost in Translation*, which was filmed at the Park Hyatt Tokyo Hotel (floors 39 to 52).

G

SHINJUKU GYOEN NATIONAL GARDEN

Located between Shinjuku and Shibuya, this site spans 144 acres and includes a Japanese garden, an English garden, and a French garden. Don't miss the cherry blossoms: The grounds contain 1,300 cherry trees of 65 different species.

H

KABUKICHO

Known as the city that never sleeps, Kabukicho is more than just a hotspot for nightlife. It also offers numerous other attractions, including theaters, arcades, and electronics stores. There's even a multilevel shopping center selling clothing, novelties, household items, and more.

I

GOLDEN GAI

This district is known for its cramped alleys and tiny two-story buildings built so close together that they almost touch. On the ground floors are cozy bars; the upstairs areas have been made into tiny apartments or other small spaces accessed by steep stairs.

J

GODZILLA STATUE

In the Kabukicho district, you can see the life-size Godzilla head up close on Godzilla Terrace in the Hotel Gracery Shinjuku, the same building that houses Toho Cinemas (which boasts an IMAX 3D screen).

K

SENSO-JI TEMPLE

Also known as Asakusa Kannon, this temple in the Asakusa district is the oldest temple in Tokyo and one of the most important pilgrimage sites in Japan.

L

YUNIKA VISION

Since 2010, this commercial building has broadcast information and advertisements continuously from 7 a.m. to 1 a.m. on three giant LED screens, each measuring 1,075 square feet. All videos include sound.

M

MEIJI MEMORIAL MUSEUM

This museum is dedicated to Emperor Meiji and his era. Visitors are treated to a large collection of historical and artistic artifacts that tell the story of the emperor's life, reign, and influence on the development of modern Japan.

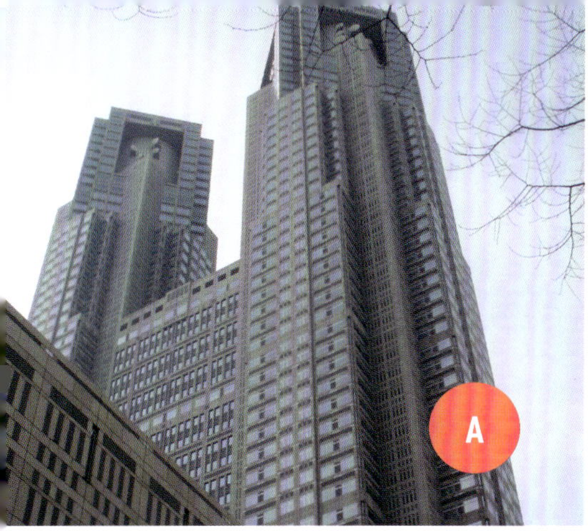
A

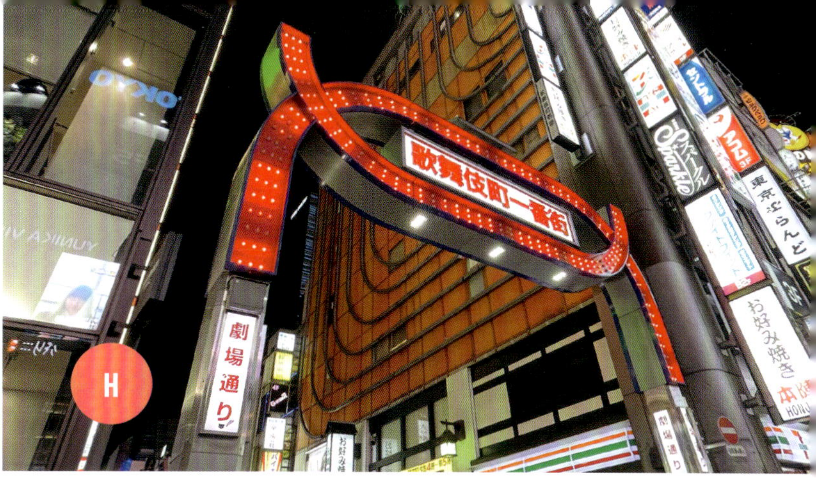
H
歌舞伎町一番街
劇場通り

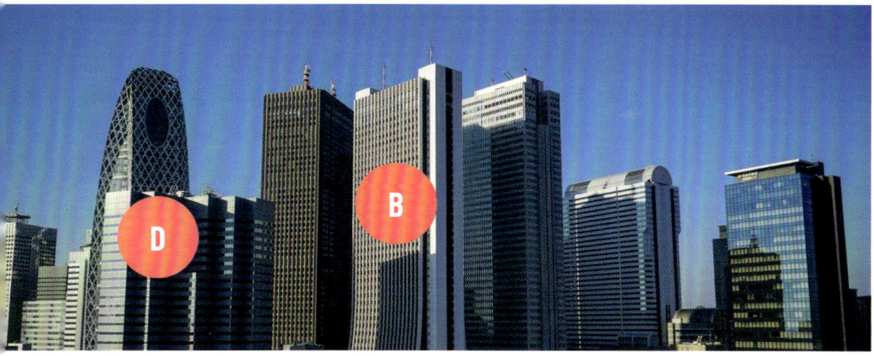
D
B

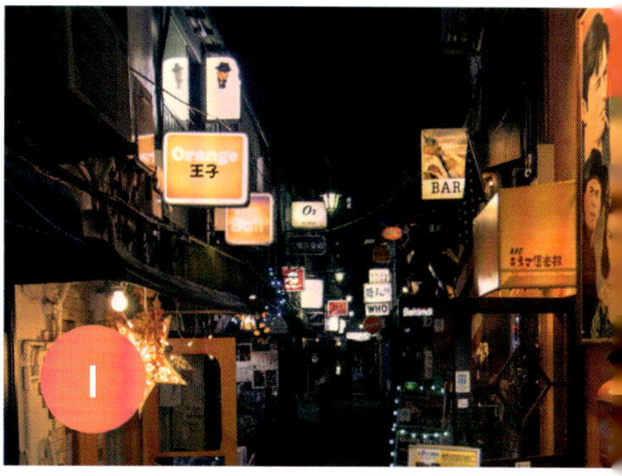
I
Orange
王子
BAR

E

J
HOTEL
新たな「アベンジャーズ」へと続く、
マーベル・スタジオ最新作!

C

F

L
SPORTS
DEPO
Alpen
Outdoors
YUNIKA VISION

G

M

K

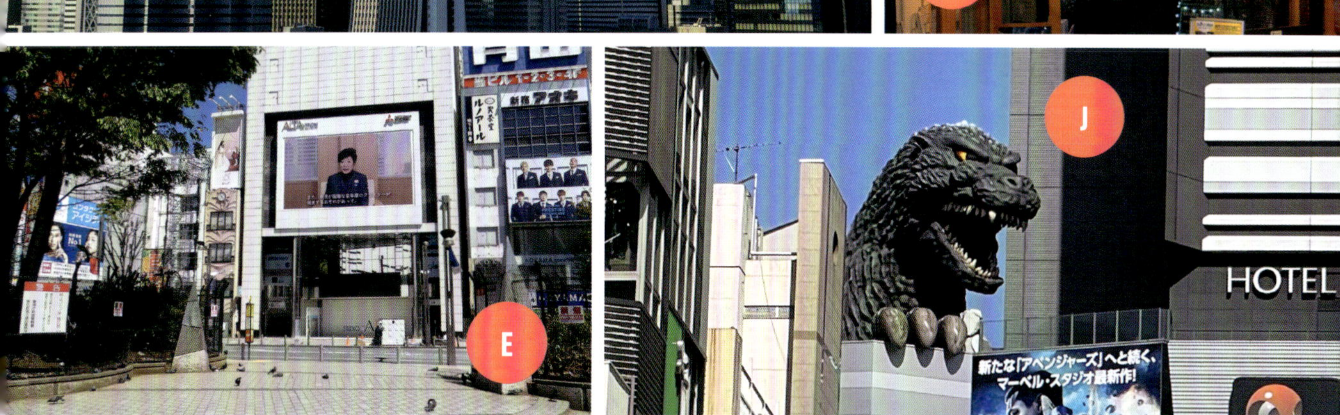

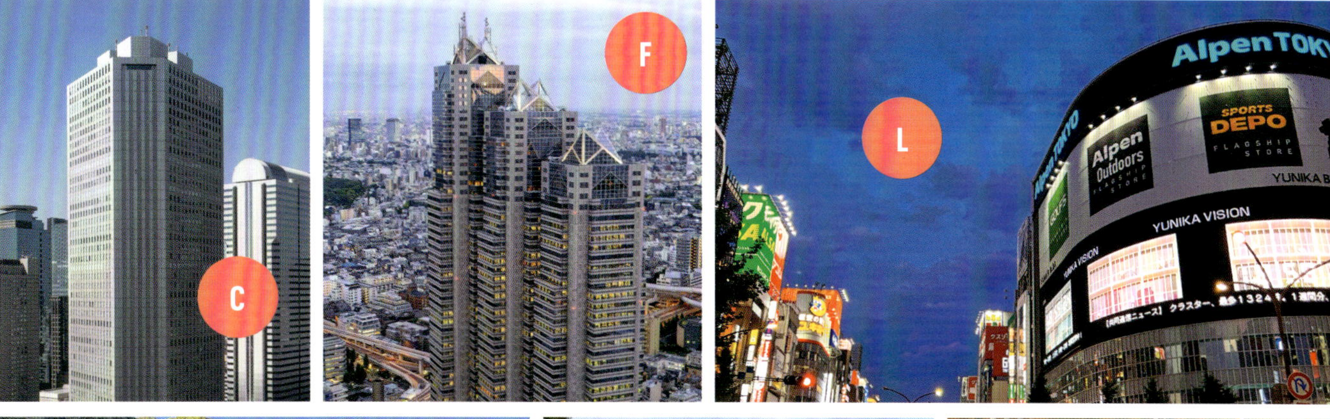

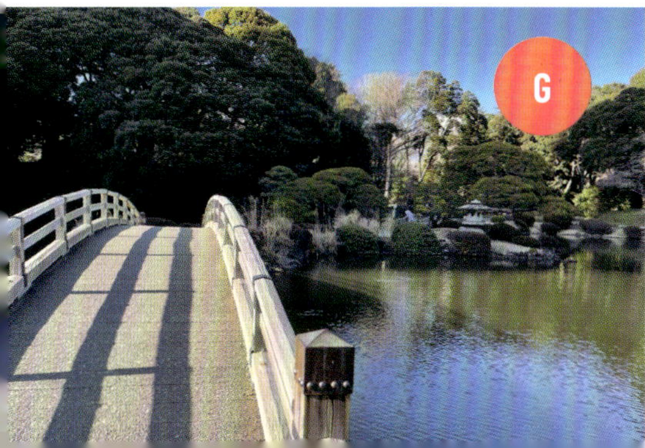

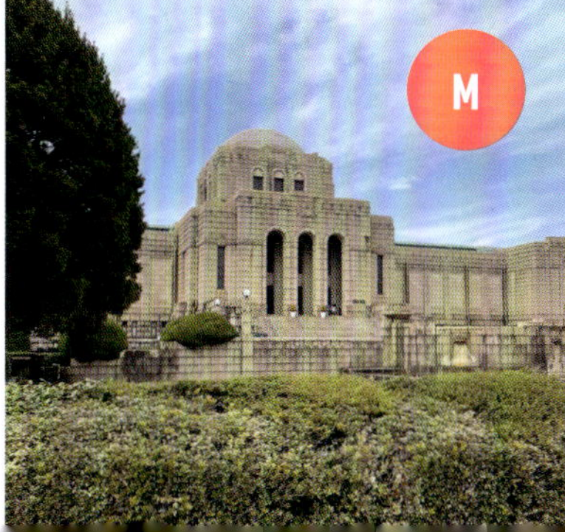

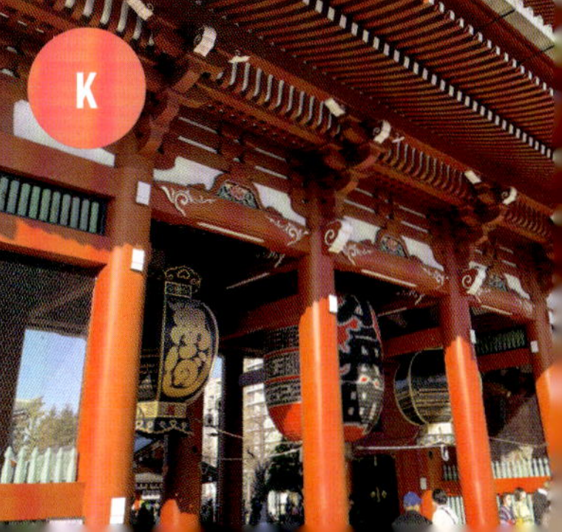

N

JAPAN NATIONAL STADIUM

Built in 2020 for the Tokyo Olympic and Paralympic Games, this stadium seats sixty-eight thousand fans. Its unique structure combines modern and traditional Japanese construction techniques, using seventy thousand cubic feet of Ryukyu pine and cedar that were transported to Tokyo from all forty-seven prefectures of Japan.

O

NTT DOCOMO YOYOGI TOWER

This tower, owned by the telecommunications company NTT Docomo, was completed in 2000 mainly to house technical facilities. A giant fifty-foot-diameter clock was installed in 2002 for NTT Docomo's tenth anniversary, making it the tallest clock tower in the world at the time.

P

SHIBUYA INTERSECTION

Called the world's busiest intersection because of the constant flow of pedestrians and traffic, this crossing is used by tens of thousands of people every day.

Q

OMOTESANDO

This fashion district is famous for the luxury clothing stores and beauty salons along its main avenue.

8

MEIJI SHRINE

This Shinto shrine located in Shibuya ward was built in honor of Emperor Meiji and Empress Shoken. It was dedicated in 1920 and reconstructed in 1958 after it was damaged during World War II.

S

TAKESHITA DORI

Young people flock to this quarter-mile pedestrian street filled with flashy stores. The street is a fashion hotspot and one of the birthplaces of the *kawaii* aesthetic.

T

NATIONAL ART CENTER TOKYO

The NACT is a modern art museum with a permanent collection of nineteenth- and twentieth-century paintings, but its main mission is to connect contemporary art with pop culture.

U

ROPPONGI HILLS MORI TOWER

This fifty-four-story skyscraper consists of offices, restaurants, and shops. It includes a panoramic observatory on the fifty-second floor and an aquarium on the fifty-fourth floor. The Mori Art Museum occupies floors 49 to 54.

V

TOKYO TOWER

Located in the Minato ward of Tokyo, Tokyo Tower is a symbol of the city. Completed in 1958, it stands 1,093 feet tall and is a popular tourist attraction. The tower won the Good Design Award in 2018.

W

RAINBOW BRIDGE

This double-decker suspension bridge connects the artificial island of Odaiba to the city of Tokyo. You can cross on foot or by car.

X

FUJI TELEVISION NETWORK

One of Tokyo's four main television networks, Fuji Television broadcasts programs and news to various regions. In addition to traditional broadcasting, it owns satellite channels that include Fuji TV One, Fuji TV Two, and Fuji TV Next.

Y

DAIKANRANSHA FERRIS WHEEL

The world's tallest Ferris wheel at the time of its inauguration in 1999, the site was closed in 2022 as part of a redevelopment plan.

Z

NIPPON BUDOKAN ARENA

This martial arts hall located in Tokyo's Kitanomaru Park was built to promote and encourage the practice of traditional Japanese martial arts. It also serves as a sports venue and multipurpose event center.

AA

GINZA WAKO

Ginza Wako is a renowned luxury store specializing in watches, jewelry, and other high-end items, located at the Ginza 4-Chome intersection. The store's iconic symbol is the clock tower on the main building, which chimes every hour during business hours.

P

V

Z

U

T

Y

W

N

O

AA

X

Q

8

S